A PLEASURE IN SCOTTISH TREES

Dedicated with love to Barbara, Meg, Janet, Sandy, John, Graham, Clare, Sam, Lily, William, Callum, Joe and Flora.

A Pleasure in Scottish Trees

Alistair Scott
Illustrations by Heather Insh

MAINSTREAM
PUBLISHING

EDINBURGH AND LONDON

First published in Great Britain in 2002 by
MAINSTREAM PUBLISHING COMPANY (EDINBURGH) LTD
7 Albany Street
Edinburgh EH1 3UG

ISBN 1 84018 568 6

A catalogue record for this book is available from the British Library

Typeset in Garamond
Printed and bound in Great Britain by
Creative Print Design Wales

CONTENTS

THE RESTORATION OF NATIVE WOODLAND

TRADITIONAL ESTATES

SOME CLASSIC SITES OF PLANTATION FORESTRY

PARTICULAR BROADLEAVES

APPROXIMATE SITE LOCATIONS

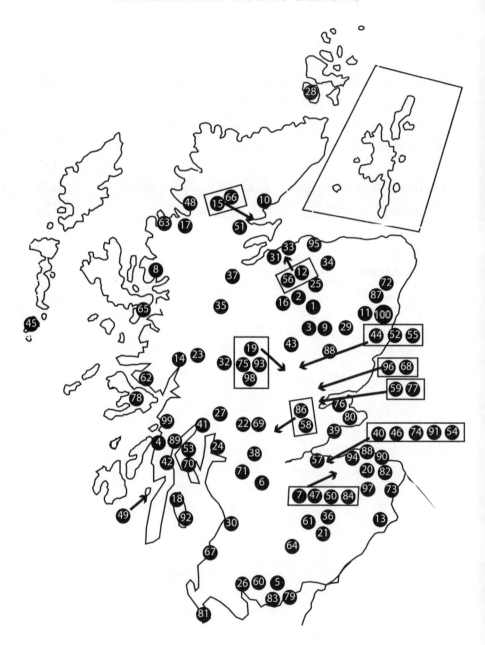

FOREWORD

The Trustees of the Scottish Forestry Trust, in seeing an earlier version of this manuscript, considered that it should be made available to a much wider audience. The text comprises a delightful collection of Alistair Scott's observations and anecdotes of individual 'tree sites' throughout Scotland. The Trustees agreed with Alistair's view that commissioning Heather Insh to provide line drawings would enhance the publication. The drawings enrich this publication in accurately portraying distinctive features that would not always be achieved easily through photography. Line drawings were therefore commissioned for 22 sites and these have been supplemented with a collection of colour photographs.

The Scottish Forestry Trust is a charitable trust established in 1983 to promote research, education and training in forestry. The Trust, in providing financial support to provide the line drawings and editing of this book, saw this publication as an important educational project in which not only people who are interested in trees but a wider public might be enticed to go out and discover these landscape treasures. Woodlands and trees contribute much of interest both in the countryside and in urban areas, while also enhancing quality of life.

I recognise that the author's enthusiasm and knowledge are infectious and I am sure that you, like me, will be stimulated to go and visit these trees. However, it should be recognised that these are only a sample selected by Alistair and there are many others which some might argue are on a par with these and equally worthy of visiting. Although our native tree flora in Scotland is poor, we have a very rich heritage of introduced trees, many of which survive and grow surprisingly well and can be found throughout most of Scotland. In commending this book I see it opening a new and delightful pastime for some people and revealing these specimen trees in a new light for others.

Sir Michael Strang Steel Bt CBE
Chairman, The Scottish Forestry Trust

INTRODUCTION

The text of *A Pleasure in Scottish Trees* was written under a personal award from The Millennium Forest for Scotland Trust (MFST). In the early months of 2001, 300 copies were printed by Dupliquick of Edinburgh and distributed as an unexpected gift to each of the Members of the Scottish Parliament, to the Chief Executives of all the organisations involved in rural Scotland and so forth. The format was pleasantly serviceable, enlivened by out-of-copyright engravings of trees which I photocopied from a book in the Herbarium Library (part of the Royal Botanic Garden Edinburgh) and Sandy Graham of Dupliquick arranged with his own fair hands.

I set out in that version my indebtedness to a wonderfully rich and varied body of people who got drawn into the project. All are, I hope, again thanked under 'Acknowledgements' but I must repeat here my special thanks to the Trust for giving me the award, to Ernest Law and Gillian McNeill, who administered the award with good humoured efficiency and to Professor T.C. Smout of St Andrews University, who was my mentor for the award, an imaginative requirement of the MFST. I had not had a mentor in my life before and greatly enjoyed and benefited from the experience.

I wish also to repeat here my particular thanks to the following who, from their different perspectives, suggested what might be included. They were Karen Chambers, Christopher Dingwall of the Garden History Society, David Henderson-Howat, Chief Conservator, Forestry Commission National Office for Scotland, Bill Mason, Principal

Silviculturist (North), Forest Research, James McCarthy, Graham Tuley and Peter Quelch, Forestry Commission Native Woodland Advisor. They will appreciate that the main difficulty was in deciding what to leave out.

A number of recipients of the booklet spoke pleasantly about the content to the point where I thought I should offer it to Mainstream and was very pleased when they accepted. A major consideration in my mind was that this would be an opportunity for the text to be supported by illustration, particularly line drawings, which have always seemed to me, when well done, the most telling, immediate, subtle and human of tree likenesses. I am delighted with the tree portraits that Heather Insh has produced and am most grateful to the Scottish Forestry Trust whose generous support for the book has been a major factor in its existence. Dr David Rook, Director of the Trust, has been particularly helpful. The photographs are my own.

Jim Paterson from Nairn again cast his highly knowledgeable eye over the text. It has also received friendly and rigorous edits from another good friend, Dr Gerald France, and from Ailsa Bathgate of Mainstream. This does not relieve me of responsibility for residual errors.

Alistair Scott
Edinburgh
November 2001

ACKNOWLEDGEMENTS

I start, as everyone who writes about trees in Scotland must start, with the late Alan Mitchell. He was not only an outstanding dendrologist but a silviculturist to his fingertips. Thinking in terms of origin, provenance, climatic match, geology, geomorphology, soils, elevation, aspect, vegetation and so forth came as naturally to him as breathing.

As it did to Professor Mark L. Anderson, whom I was surprised and pleased to find turning up frequently in these pages as I remembered what he taught me about Scotland, trees, silviculture and ways of seeing. Memorably, he failed a student for proposing, in a dummy management plan, to plant Sitka spruce in Cawdor Old Wood. 'Have you learnt nothing?' he is alleged to have said.

As the project progressed it was extraordinary and highly pleasurable to see how many other people got drawn in, to contribute their expertise or perspective. My thanks therefore to the following, with apologies to any inadvertently omitted:

David Alderman, TROBI, Bedford
Crinan Alexander, BFT
Sir Ralph Anstruther of that Ilk Bt, Balkaskic
Dr Philip Ashmole, BFT
Dick Balharry, Newtonmore
Jim and Suzann Barr, Abriachan Forest Trust
Derek Beavis, RBGE
Jane Begg, Woodland Trust, Glen Finglas

John Bell, Dunnikier, Falkirk
Dr Erica Benson, Botany Department, University of Abertay Dundee
Peter Bickmore Dundas, SNH, Edinburgh
Dr John Blyth, University of Edinburgh (retired)
Ewan Cameron, SNH, Deeside
Mr and Mrs Nigel Champion, Cairnsmore, Newton Stewart
Hugh Clayden, Forest District Manager, Forest Enterprise, Aberfoyle
Dr Joan Cottrell, Northern Research Station, Forest Research, Bush
Peter Cox, Glendoick, Perthshire
Sandy Cram, Forestry Commission, Banchory (retired)
The Earl of Cromartie, Castle Leod, Strathpeffer
Peter Darling, Head Forester, Lothian Estates, Jedburgh
Professor Jim Dickson, Department of Botany, University of Glasgow
Duncan Donald, Garden Advisor, NTS, Edinburgh
Althea Dundas Bekker, Arniston, Midlothian
Bob Dunsmore, Conservator, Highland Conservancy, Forestry Commission
Peter Dyer, Carpenter, Stornoway Castle Estates
Keith Fairclough, RSPB, Orkney
Charlie Fleming, Head Forester, Meikleour
Dr Alan Fletcher, Forestry Commission (retired)
Douglas Foreman, Strutt and Parker, Banchory
Ian Fraser, School of Scottish Studies, University of Edinburgh
Martin Gardner, Conifer Conservation Programme, RBGE
Shona Glen, SNH, Newton Stewart
Ted Green, Windsor Great Park
John Halliday, SNH, Lochgilphead
Alan Harrison, Northern Research Station, Forest Research, Bush
Kate Holl, SNH, Edinburgh
Dr Peter Hopkins, Cree Valley Woodlands, Newton Stewart
Syd House, Conservator, Perth Forestry Commission
Karen Hay, Edinburgh Urban Forestry Project
Dr Ian Hulbert, Scottish Agricultural College, Kirkton Farm, Crianlarich

Acknowledgements

Thomas Huxley, Pitcairngreen, Perthshire
James Hunter Blair, Blairquhan, Ayrshire
Hugh Insley, Director, North Scotland, Forest Enterprise
Andrew Jones, Scottish Wildlife Trust, Cumbernauld
Erica Knott, SNH, Newton Stewart
Chris Langton, Woods Manager, Atholl Estates (retired)
Dr R.G. Law, Gatehouse of Fleet
Alan Leitch, SNH, Dalkeith
Dr Philip Lusby, RBGE
Dr Derek Lyddon, Edinburgh
Cameron Manson, Head Ranger, Dalkeith Country Park
Duncan MacAlpine, Head Gardener, Brechin Castle
Willie McGhee, BFT
Linda McGinley, Private Woodlands, Forestry Commission, Edinburgh
Donald Mackay, The Scottish Office (retired)
Malcolm McNeill, Head Gardener, Achamore, Gigha
Simon McPhun, Head Gardener, Inverewe
Niall MacPherson, Barra
Dr Douglas Malcolm, University of Edinburgh (retired)
Andrew Matheson, Brahan
Paul Matthews, Glasgow Botanic Gardens
Wendy and John Mattingley, Cluny House, Aberfeldy
David Miller, SNH, Kinlochewe
David Mitchell, Kirkcudbright
Andrew Nicol, Ballogie Estate, Deeside
Mike Osborne, Roslin
Mike Phillips, Newton, Elgin
Louise Pinckney, Head Gardener, Armadale Castle, Isle of Skye
Callum Pirnie, Head Gardener, NTS, Crathes
Ian Pollock, Cumbernauld
Nigel Price, Head Gardener, Brodick, Isle of Arran
Beatrix Richards, Forestry Policy Officer, WWF, London
Mary Robertson, Ranger, Hopetoun House Trust, South Queensferry

Philip Rolfe, General Manager, Dunkeld House Hotel
Frances Scott, NTS, Broughton House, Kirkcudbright
John Sinclair, Royal Scottish Forestry Trust, Cashel
Mike Smith, BFT
Geoffrey Stell, Historic Scotland, Edinburgh
Neil Sutherland, Architect, Inverness
Mike Swift, Head Gardener, Torosay Castle, Isle of Mull
Fraser Symonds, SNH, Golspie
Colin Taylor, Cambusmore Estate, Sutherland
Crawford Taylor, Head Forester, Scone Palace, Perth
Jenny Taylor, Farming Forestry Wildlife Advisory Group, Orkney
Stewart Taylor, Reserve Manager, RSPB, Abernethy
Ainslie Thin, Edinburgh
Dr Richard Tipping, University of Stirling
Barry Unwin, Curator, Logan Botanic Garden, Wigtownshire
Philip Whitfield, Forest District Manager, Forest Enterprise, Moray
Peter Winfield, Edinburgh
Dr Rick Worrell, Aberfeldy
Iain Young, SNH, Edinburgh

CREDO

Somewhat to my surprise I have a *Credo* about trees in Scotland. It is this.

Scotland's native trees, numbering between 14 and 21, depending on your definition of tree, are, species for species, as good as any in the world. In particular, considered either for their beauty or their utility, Scots pine, sessile oak and silver birch are out of the top drawer. Sadly, woodlands of native trees descended from the 'wildwood' have been massively reduced from, perhaps, 70 per cent of the land surface at their maximum extent to less than 2 per cent today. As the maximum extent existed 5,000 years ago and under a different climate such a comparison may not be particularly useful, but most people agree that there should be a great deal more, particularly in regions like the Borders or Fife where woodlands are scarce to vanishing point. Efforts over the last decade or so, to create or recreate native woods are admirable.

It seems like common sense to me that if, at some point in its life, you can use some of the trees in a wood as timber without compromising other objectives, you should do so. If you can grow an oak, a pine or a birch, which looks good, houses all the relevant wildlife *and* is straight and clean of branches, then go for it. They do so in Finland and Austria.

Due to the vagaries of continental drift and glaciation our tree flora is distinctly thin in comparison to many places, especially the temperate zones of North America, the Himalayas, China, Japan and Chile. It is not that the Scottish climate is unsuited to growing trees, quite the opposite in fact. A case can be made that, as a result of the Gulf Stream, Scotland has one of the best climates on earth, outside the tropics, for growing a wide range of trees. Scotsmen roamed the world throughout the last two centuries sending home seeds and plants from all over the globe with the result that there are well over 1,000 introduced tree species growing happily somewhere in Scotland.

The native tree flora conspicuously lacks, of the world's great timber trees, a spruce, a fir, a larch, a beech and a maple. We have gained, or should have gained, immeasurably from the arrival here of Sitka spruce, Douglas fir, European larch, common beech and sycamore. Between them and our native timbers we have a better resource base than anywhere in northern Europe and as good as any in central Europe. Our timber industry is now as high tech as any in the world and supplies 26 per cent of our sawn softwood demand, but almost entirely from Sitka spruce, as we are failing to make the best possible use of these other, potentially valuable timbers.

Recognition of the value of these introduced species is not to argue that the effects of their arrival on our landscape have been everywhere benign. Sitka spruce was planted in too many places where no trees should be. It was, and to some extent still is, too often cultivated like a field of wheat, not as a complex forest. Sycamore is usually best kept out of nature reserves, and so on. But we have only had a century or two in which to experience these new trees and the lessons have already been learnt, or most of them have.

The numerous introduced trees that we use in our streets and parks and gardens are not without blemish. I could do without the strawberry-pink Kanzan cherry, for example, or that diseased-looking, variegated poplar. But this is to cavil. Overall, introduced trees are wonderfully enriching. It is always an interesting exercise to imagine what our towns and cities would look like stripped of all but the few native trees. They would be distinctly bare.

Knowledge, and knowledgeable use, of garden trees is increasing, thanks in large measure to the superb examples out there such as Crarae,

Crathes, Inverewe, Arduaine, Brechin Castle, Falkland Palace, Glendoick, Innes, Torosay, Cluny House, Tyninghame, to say nothing of the Botanic Gardens, not only those clustered round the Royal Botanic Garden Edinburgh, but also those in Aberdeen, St Andrews, Dundee and Glasgow.

Trees must be chosen so that they fit the purpose. The old estates knew all about that. You moved from garden trees to policy trees, through parkland trees to the arboretum and, often via fragments of native oakwood or birchwood, to the productive forest. There are still splendid examples like Cawdor, Atholl, Drumlanrig, Brahan and Blairquhan.

Unfortunately, educationally and institutionally, at local, regional and national level, this approach has, more usually than not, been fragmented. Forestry was separated from arboriculture, separated from the management of semi-natural woodlands and absolutely separated from gardening. Foresters did not know the price of a sheep. Farmers could not identify a Douglas fir. There are now, however, encouraging signs of a shift back to an overall understanding. The Forestry Commission in all its guises has moved massively towards the centre during the last few decades. Even the Royal Society for the Protection of Birds (RSPB) has been heard to mutter that Scots pine timber may not be a bad thing in the long run.

Finally, I like wood: wooden houses, wooden barns, oak roofs, pine telegraph poles, cedar shingles, clinker-built boats, picnic benches, tables, chairs, axe-handles, chopping boards, bowls, spoons, spurtles, totem poles, Morris Travellers, Russian dolls. I delight in the way that every culture has put its trees to appropriate uses. It is a universal source of pleasure. How satisfactory it would be if we could reconnect the trees growing out there with the wood that pleases us in here. How fulfilling, if we could start to innovate for our own twenty-first-century needs. Hence my admiration for the Wood School at Ancrum, Jedburgh: half a dozen young designers and craftsmen in wood, sharing the expensive machinery. If we are going to be better Europeans, could we not be Scandinavian in our use and appreciation of wood?

INTRODUCTORY NOTES

IDENTIFICATION: Although I say a good deal about the appearance of trees, this is not a manual of tree identification. There are excellent books available for that purpose. Beware the highly coloured. It is difficult to be sure of identity on the basis of even the sharpest colour photographs. To my mind the best field guide is still Alan Mitchell's *Trees of Britain*, 1974. I am on my third copy, the first two having succumbed to book fatigue, from too much field use.

MEASUREMENTS: I am of the generation that learnt the poetry of miles, furlongs, poles, chains, yards, feet, inches and hoppus feet per acre. We then had to teach ourselves Napoleonic measures, logical but shadowless. In what follows I have bowed to hectares and kilometres but reneged over tree measurement, where you will find the traditional feet and inches still installed. It makes for immediate comparison with earlier records.

OPENING TIMES: I have not tried to be specific about the opening months and hours of any of the properties discussed. Each year that information may differ slightly. It is readily acquired from tourist centres, or from the Scotland's Gardens Scheme booklet. On private land it is a basic courtesy to ask permission. I have only once been refused. Everywhere else I have found a most pleasant welcome.

ORDERING THE ENTRIES: There is no entirely satisfactory way of ordering lists of trees. The standard botanical ordering is irritating if you don't know what is being ordered. Alphabetically by English name results in curious juxtapositions. I have chosen to list the individual trees alphabetically by Latin name, separating the conifers from the broadleaves. At least this keeps the pines, say, or the oaks together.

ABBREVIATIONS: A number of organisations and designations appear so frequently that I have thought it helpful to use abbreviations. I hope I am right. They are:

BFT: Borders Forest Trust
MFST: Millennium Forest for Scotland Trust
NCC: Nature Conservancy Council
NNR: National Nature Reserve
NTS: National Trust for Scotland
RBGE: Royal Botanic Garden Edinburgh
RSFS: Royal Scottish Forestry Society
RSPB: Royal Society for the Protection of Birds
SNH: Scottish Natural Heritage
SSSI: Site of Special Scientific Interest
TROBI: Tree Register of the British Isles
WWF: World Wildlife Fund

NATIVE WOODLANDS

1. THE NATIVE PINEWOODS
(See first photo section)

I had my first experience of a native pinewood, indeed of anywhere north of Edinburgh, in 1949. We camped on the south shore of Loch Rannoch with the edge of the Black Wood of Rannoch a pine cone's throw away. Was it then or was it later I learned that the wood was 'black' because the trees were dark pines in contrast to light oaks and that the pines preferred these colder, north-facing slopes while the oaks relished the sun? My abiding memory of that first visit, apart from the big granny pines, was finding a vicious spring-trap set to catch a wildcat by hanging a large, very-dead fish from a tree above it. We sprang the trap with a thick branch. I can still hear the echo of the sound in my memory.

A year later, Dr 'Jock' Carlisle of the Department of Forestry, University of Aberdeen, began the six years of field investigations that were to result in the defining book he wrote in collaboration with Professor H.M. Steven, entitled *The Native Pinewoods of Scotland*. It includes all pinewoods they believed to be directly descended by natural regeneration from the post-glacial forest. The preface is dated April 1957. First publication was 1959. It is worth remembering that the Forestry Commissioners gave 'generous financial support'. It is a scholarly work and good reading. Perhaps no words written about the pinewoods have had more impact than these: 'To walk through . . . gives one a better idea of what a primeval forest was like than can be got from any other woodland scene in Britain . . . to stand in them is to feel the past.'

Steven and Carlisle recognised 35 pinewoods, in 8 geographical groups, totalling about 12,000 ha. A careful new survey, done for the Forestry Commission by Graham Tuley while he was Highland Native Woodland Advisor, subdivided and added to this number so that the Pinewood Inventory now has 77 entries in 7 biochemical regions totalling about 16,000 ha. A further analysis has brought the total to 17,882 ha but that merely underlines how difficult it is to measure any natural population.

The native woodlands can be found within an area defined by: furthest north, Loch Assynt; furthest west, Shieldaig; furthest south, Glen Falloch, by Crianlarich; furthest east, Glen Ferrick, Deeside. Half the area is within five pinewoods: Abernethy and Rothiemurchus in Strathspey, Glen Tanar on Deeside, Glen Affric in the west and the Black Wood of Rannoch. Many are tiny but no less valuable for that.

Elsewhere I write about some mishandling of pinewoods in the 1960s and 1970s but all that is in the past. Thanks to enlightened policies, practices and resourcing by the land-owning and grant-awarding arms of the Forestry Commission and to many, many others in the pinewoods equation, the future of these national treasures seems more secure than it has ever been.

For anyone interested in the process of change, the most easily accessible critical texts are the proceedings of the Pinewood Conferences at Aviemore in 1975 and at Inverness in 1994. More difficult to find are the newsletters of the Native Woodlands Discussion Group starting in autumn 1974. Who can say why and when opinions are changed, but I will always raise my glass to this relaxed, informal group and to Rawdon Goodier, then of the Nature Conservancy Council (NCC), who was so influential in its existence and ethos.

2. ABERNETHY RESERVE, NETHYBRIDGE
Royal Society for the Protection of Birds
Open

The Pinewood Conference at Aviemore in 1975 was a pivotal moment for me, as, considering what followed, it must have been for many others. Rereading the conference papers reminds me of their quality and the mood of the occasion. The turning point was the excursion to Abernethy when I realised with dismay that the forest-management companies involved, driven as they had to be by considerations of tax and profit on behalf of their pension-fund owners, could not be entrusted with the management of these native pinewoods. What they were doing seemed unacceptable, yet they had the support of the Forestry Commission locally. Looking back, it is clear that the national conservation legislation and agreements then in place were inadequate.

We will need a bundle of internal NCC reports and probably some cabinet papers to unravel exactly what happened next. Suffice it to say that the RSPB, with major NCC grant aid, bought a big chunk of pinewoods around Abernethy. They have subsequently extended their Speyside holding hugely, taking in some of the high ground of the Cairngorms. To my mind, their management has been exemplary, much to the credit of Stewart Taylor, who has been at Abernethy from the beginning and Reserve Manager for the past 12 years.

Clearly it makes for a simpler life if your overriding objective of management is to develop or modify habitat, woodland and non-woodland, for the benefit of birds, with scant concern for the production of timber and, although there are many visitors, no concern for the promotion of public recreation. In this way you avoid the tricky balancing act of the neighbouring Rothiemurchus estate. However, an enlarging, varied bird population implies a varied habitat for many other things, including the uncharismatic tooth fungi, parasitic wasps and, my favourites, the slime moulds. Stewart Taylor happily accepts the proposition that his organisation is moving towards becoming the Royal

Society for the Protection of Biodiversity. The woods also look very good.

Central to the success of Abernethy is the reduction in deer numbers and the concomitant removal of deer fences. Numbers are now below the Fraser Darling formula of six per square kilometre. Pine, birch and other seedlings are beginning to appear not only on the periphery of the woods but also much further out. It is not unexpected. Professor Smout's authoritative examination of the history of Rothiemurchus demonstrates the willingness of Speyside pinewoods to regenerate in the absence of significant grazing. There is a notional worry that an overvigorous woody-shrub-layer may be inhibiting to tree seedlings or to the success of woodland grouse, but it remains notional. A degree of grazing is necessary. Deer may be sufficient. If not, cattle or even pigs are under consideration.

Professor Smout has also demonstrated that, historically, woods with marketplace value have been more secure and more robust than those without. I am not convinced that the RSPB will remain uniquely immune to the buffeting of the economic world that affects the rest of us and believe they may yet find a sawmill an essential (and compatible) part of their management.

3. MAR LODGE, BRAEMAR
The National Trust for Scotland
Open

Before the early 1990s, most Scots, if they had heard of Mar Lodge at all, knew it as the place bought by the larger-than-life Gerard Panchaud in 1962 for £100,000 to develop a hotel, or bought unseen for £7 million in 1989 by John Kluge, 'the second richest man in America', for his colourful wife Patricia. Hillwalkers knew the estate as the route through to the Cairngorms from the Braemar side. Forest conservationists knew it, thanks to Steven and Carlisle, as the location of a pinewood decimated in the period 1750–1850, with virtually no regeneration since then because priority had been given to red deer.

Purchase by the National Trust for Scotland (NTS) in 1995 has changed all that. The purchase and events to date have been interestingly written up by J. Laughton Johnston. Much credit to the NTS that they agreed his proposal, gave him access to staff and management plans and did not seek any editorial input.

The purchase of Mar Lodge doubled the land holding of the NTS. Funding for the purchase price of £5.6 million came from the National Heritage Memorial Fund – £1.5 million (together with an endowment of £8.7 million), and from the Easter Charitable Trust – £4 million. To the annoyance of many people, the Easter Charitable Trust was initially anonymous. It was generally guessed to be a consortium of Scottish landowning interests since who else, it was asked, in offering £4 million unsolicited, would make a condition, *inter alia*, that: 'The NTS shall manage the Estate so as to conserve its valuable, ecological and landscape features in harmony with its maintenance as a Highland Sporting Estate for so long as field sports remain legal.' In January 2002, however, it was revealed that the benefactor was Ann Marie Salvesen, the philanthropic heiress of the shipping dynasty.

Some think that the NTS should have walked away from such a condition. Others see it as an opportunity to work towards a balance of interests, which, if successful, may have major 'domino' impacts on private owner management across a wide area.

Mar Lodge Estate is a great deal more than a pinewood. Indeed the 836 ha of woodland is only a small percentage of the whole 29,500 ha. However, success or failure in the management of the pinewood will be viewed particularly critically. Nixon and Cameron suggest a mean age for the pines of 226 years with a range of between 132 and 352 years. They also found that the 'majority of the trees might be expected to produce good quantities of viable seed for at least a further 100 years'. It is the present intention to proceed only by natural regeneration. There was common agreement that the deer population at purchase, *circa* 3,500, was too high. A target total population of 1,650, comprising 950 hinds and 700 stags, was set for the year 2000. The present number is stated by Alister Clunes, NTS manager, to be *circa* 2,600. 'We had aimed at a greater reduction, but this proved difficult, especially with hinds.'

It was a brave decision for the NTS to become engaged with Mar Lodge. It will be a long, long time before any of us can come to an informed view about the wisdom of their engagement. By that time, the political and economic climate will, as always, be unrecognisable.

4. TAYNISH WOODS
NATIONAL NATURE RESERVE, TAYVALLICH, ARGYLL
Scottish Natural Heritage
Open

All authorities agree that some 5,000 years ago most of Scotland, except the high tops, the wettest marshes and perhaps some of the far north mainland, was covered with woodland, though not all of it dense.

In his latest and best attempt at assessing the present area of semi-natural woodlands, Neil MacKenzie arrives at a total of about 152,000 ha, and only a little more planted woodland containing native species. In round figures these make up 2 per cent of the land surface of Scotland. Of the semi-natural, 40 per cent is birchwood, 20 per cent is pinewood and 20 per cent or about 30,000 ha, is upland oakwood. In 1977 Derek Ratcliffe, then Chief Scientist for the NCC, edited the *Nature Conservation Review: A selection of biological sites of national importance to nature conservation in Britain.* It seemed remarkable at the time for the width, depth and clarity of its analysis. In retrospect it seems an astonishing tour de force: the most powerful and prescient statement of conservation concern in Britain during the twentieth century.

Ratcliffe graded sites as 1 or 2, probably unwisely, but that is another story. Among the Grade 1 oakwoods in Scotland he included the Loch Lomond islands, Dinnet Oakwood in Aberdeenshire, the Pass of Killiecrankie, Coille Ardura on Mull and Ariundle, Salen-Strontian, Glen Nant and Taynish, all in the west. The choice was subjective. These days the choice is intended to be objective, or quasi-objective: examining size, diversity, naturalness, history, potential value, landscape, public use, education and interpretation. By either route Taynish gets top marks. The NCC acquired 327 ha in 1973.

There are presently 71 National Nature Reserves (NNRs). All are under review. Taynish is one of the score given the green light at first sieve and the reasons are clear. It is large and remarkably intact, probably because its parallel strips of rock and hollow were unsuitable for cultivation. It is surrounded by delectable valley mires: rough fields which are home to the Marsh Fritillary butterfly, saltings and rich sea lochs. It is brimming over with a flora and fauna unique to the clean, warm, moist climate of the west coast. Since it contains 'habitat types and species which are rare or threatened in a European context', it is a candidate Special Area of Conservation (SAC) under the European Habitats Directive (92/43/EEC).

But forget all that. Just think of it as a delicious place to be alive, especially on a sunny morning in September, if possible in the company of John Halliday, Reserves Manager, particularly if there is a swarm of Clouded Yellow butterflies. Biodiversity may be an abstract scientific concept but it is also, perhaps pre-eminently, something to which all the human senses respond.

5. THE FLEET WOODLANDS
GATEHOUSE OF FLEET, GALLOWAY
Various owners – *see text*
Carstramon and Forest Enterprise woods open, the others not

The Fleet Woodlands is the collective term for a suite of mainly oakwoods running, on both sides of the river, north and south of Gatehouse of Fleet. Taken together they are, with some of the Cree woods, the best remnants of mixed, deciduous woodland left in Dumfries and Galloway – a poignant reminder of what was, once upon a time, a locally predominant land use. Some are privately owned, some belong to Forest Enterprise. The best loved is the 86 ha Carstramon (or Castramont) Wood, now in the careful ownership of the Scottish Wildlife Trust – a gift, in 1994, of the late Mrs Murray-Usher. Carstramon has been notified as a Site of Special Scientific Interest since 1968 and management of the woodlands must therefore be agreed with Scottish Natural Heritage.

The best time to visit is late May when the wood is awash with wild hyacinths, the effect all the more dramatic because the ground drops fairly sharply from the Doon of Carstramon and the vivid blue appears to flow downhill. There are big old beech trees planted on the top of the hill, perhaps 200 years old and not long for this world. There are a few substantial Scots pine, also planted; some ash in the gulleys; more birch; but the principal tree is sessile oak. Most of the documentation indicates that this is an ancient semi-natural oakwood with a history dating from the seventeenth century of management as coppice. Essentially this was, even is, a cut-and-come-again system much practised right across Britain for the production of charcoal and tan bark as well as poles and fuel. There is some documentary evidence that part of the wood was planted with acorns from England, and the presence of collapsed stone dykes suggests a phase of needing to keep beasts in, or out. Detailed research has yet to come.

In May the fresh, apple-green of the new oak leaves makes a wonderful airy tent over the blue haze from the ground and the crozier bracken fronds. Add in that at this time of year the Fleet Woodlands are loud with returning migrants – Wood Warbler, Willow Warbler, Chiffchaff, Pied Flycatcher, Redstart – and you might think that the world was young and uncomplicated.

The enjoyment of the lay public is as central to the philosophy of the Scottish Wildlife Trust as the conservation of ecologically sound habitat. At Carstramon there are unobtrusive lay-bys, footpaths, information boards and the like. Management is gentle, confined at this stage to the removal of non-native and potentially invasive species like sycamore, and beech regeneration. There are an encouraging number of oak seedlings at ankle height, though most will probably lose the battle with bracken, roe deer and shade from the existing canopy.

One of Carstramon's claims to fame is a beetle, *Trachodes hispidus*, for which this is the only known Scottish location. It is a weevil dependent on oak or beech faggots. Since there are some 3,000 species of beetle in Britain you will be forgiven for not identifying *Trachodes hispidus*, supposing you can find him, or her.

6. THE CADZOW OAKS, NEAR HAMILTON
Mr Alan Wiseman
Private except for a few trees within the Chatelherault Country
  Park. Many of the private trees are visible from the Park

There is a recent, persuasive school of thought which reckons that there is
a substantial area of wood pasture – a widespread traditional system of
land use combining trees and grazing – still visible in Scotland, if you have
the experienced eye to see through or past obscuring later uses. It helps if
you are familiar with contemporary European wood pasture systems and
what all experts agree to be the two most intact and inarguable examples

in the Scottish lowlands: the Dalkeith Old Wood and these Cadzow oaks.

A few of the remaining 370 oaks are within the Chatelherault Country Park. Most are on private land, but a good number are visible from the park. The total area covered by the trees has halved in the last 50 years, thus increasing the ecological and historical value of what remains.

Thanks to recent studies by Martin Dougall and Professor Jim Dickson of Glasgow University, drawing on earlier work at Cadzow and oak experts elsewhere, there are now provisional answers to these often-asked questions. How old are the trees? Are these pedunculate or sessile oaks?* How have they been managed? Were they planted?

All the trees are likely to be at least 550 years old and some may be as old as 750. They show more characteristics of pedunculate oak but also 'clear evidence' of sessile. If they have ever been pollarded, it has not been for a very long time. There is evidence that some were planted, but others may be remnants of a natural wood. The balance of expert opinion–guesses favours the view that most were planted, perhaps with acorns from not very far away.

The trees themselves are just what you would expect: massive, pot-bellied, stagheaded, hollow, encrusted with huge burrs and bosses, yet with new shoots and leaves fresher than paint. Thanks to a combination of the concerned owner, a professional forester, and the vigorous and rigorous attention of the local Scottish Natural Heritage (SNH) Area Officer, large numbers of acorns have been collected from the parent trees, grown-on in a nursery and planted back on site, protected against livestock and deer. Part of the area is grazed. Cattle have meanwhile been excluded from the section you see from the Park but this too will revert

---

* Two species of oak are native to Scotland, and Britain as a whole. They are, respectively, pedunculate and sessile oaks. These terms refer to the stalk or peduncle bearing the cup on which the acorn sits. On pedunculate oak the stalk is very long, 1.5 to 3 inches, and is often called a Dutchman's pipe. In sessile oak, the stalk is very short or absent, the acorn cup is said to be sessile. There are features of the leaves that will help to separate the species but both are somewhat variable. It certainly helps if there are acorns on the trees and you can reach them.

to wood pasture when it is safe to let the beasts back in. There are the usual voices raised against such bold action. I think it is admirable.

7. DALKEITH OLD WOOD, DALKEITH ESTATE
Buccleuch Estates
Open on foot, dawn to dusk

Dalkeith Old Wood is the arboreal equivalent of Dryburgh Abbey, say,

or St Margaret's Chapel or Duffus Castle: an astonishing relic of the twelfth century, except that, unlike these famous historical buildings, the wood is known only to the locals and a few hundred enthusiasts of trees, fungi, lichens, beetles, bees, wasps and the like. It seems likely that some of the trees are in direct line of descent from the post-glacial, mixed deciduous forest and, almost uniquely, the land between widely spaced trees has been grazed in one form or another since it was declared a royal hunting forest in 1163. Then, or later, it was enclosed as a deer

park by walling or fencing-off the neck of land between the rivers North and South Esk. Oliver Rackham and others have researched how this was done in England but, so far as I can determine, nobody has studied this or many other details at Dalkeith.

With the exception of a few magnificent hollies, mainly in the north-west corner, almost all the trees in the wood are oaks. In 1972, W.A. Fairbairn, known to his students as 'Snowy' Fairbairn due to his fine head of hair, reckoned that they were 70 per cent pedunculate, 22 per cent sessile and the rest intermediate. A recent, as yet unpublished, study of 400 trees by Dr Joan Cottrell of the Forestry Commission Research Branch (part of a pan-European study) shifts the balance to 95.5 per cent pedunculate, but this, by European agreement, recognises no intermediates. Fairbairn thought that sessile occupied the more freely drained soils and pedunculate the heavier. He thought that the former were native descendents of the wildwood and the pedunculate both natural and planted. All experts who have looked at the wood, including Fairbairn, George Peterken and Oliver Rackham agree that there are at least two generations of tree stems: the older dating from pre-1600, being multi-stemmed coppice pollards; the younger being 'maidens' from the seventeenth century. Fairbairn thought there was planting in 1820 and 1850, but does not cite the evidence. Rackham reckoned that a tree pollarded in *circa* 1600 could be on a stool dating back to Robert the Bruce.

Over half the trees have signs of the onset of old age and some are well advanced. Earlier woodsmen and owners, using words like diseased and moribund, hastened such veterans into firewood. Over the past decade or so, however, there has been a complete change of perspective. Now, hollowness, the antler-like appearance known as stagheading, deadwood and the like are seen as virtues, providing niches for all sorts of wildlife dependent on such exceptionally rare habitats. Perhaps the next step could be to bring in cartloads of dead trees from elsewhere to 'restock' areas from which the moribund trees were removed?

After two centuries or more without regeneration, management is now urgently directed towards ensuring a succession. Young trees, grown from acorns collected in the wood, are being planted in small stock-proof enclosures, so that the traditional cattle grazing can continue.

Put aside a morning soon, preferably in autumn, but spring, summer or winter will do fine, to walk slowly through this almost unique piece of living history. Say a silent word of thanks to generations of Buccleuchs who have resisted temptations – no doubt numerous – to 'improve'.

8. RASSAL ASHWOOD
NATIONAL NATURE RESERVE, WESTER ROSS
Managed by Scottish Natural Heritage under an agreement with
   Lochcarron Estate
Open
(See first photo section)

The most remarkable, as distinct from the most dramatic, sceneries north and west of the Great Glen, are those green pastures where the thin, discontinuous band of limestone that runs from Durness to Kishorn comes into view or influences the view. The pastures are all the more remarkable because they are sandwiched between the unforgiving Torridonian sandstone to the west and the implacable Moine flags or quartzite to the east. Suddenly, in this rugged landscape, there are wild strawberries, wood sanicle, holly-fern and the dark-red helleborine. The trout are twice the size of the Highland average.

The change is most dramatic around Durness (which gives its name to the limestone), at Inchnadamph and here at Rassal on the road south from Shieldaig to Kishorn. The 16 ha wood is just beside the road. An hour's walk along the paths will give you an immediate and satisfying sense of this, the most northerly ashwood in Britain. Better still, cross the hill from Strathcarron below Glas Bheinn and Sgurr a Gharaidh and come down on the wood via some extraordinary geological exposures, including a limestone pavement covered with mountain avens.

The conservation value of Rassal was recognised by Donald McVean in the early 1950s and it was declared an NNR in 1956. Until recently the management has been preoccupied with regeneration of the ash and attendant trees using natural regeneration and planting. There is a 2.5 ha enclosure from 1957, a 4 ha enclosure from 1975 and the whole wood was ring-fenced in 1990. A glance at the vegetation either side of a deer fence is enough to see the results. Grazing means a sward like a lawn, while the cessation of grazing means that everything grows, most obviously bracken and meadowsweet, but also plants like rowan, willow and some ash. You almost need a torch in the oldest enclosure.

So far, so good. The next phase of management is being informed by a wider scientific and historical base. Knowledge is growing not only about the populations of all the biological groups in the wood but also of their relative importance in a Scottish and European context and the conditions required to sustain them. There is a strengthening conviction that the ash trees survived not by accident but because they were relevant to earlier farmers, including, by definition, the earliest. Not only their survival but also their distribution is strongly suggestive of upland wood pasture. There is a parallel increasing awareness that the lichens dependent on the trees are of equal conservation value. With such advances in knowledge, management becomes more informed, more complex, more difficult and more interesting. Is it, as elsewhere, a matter not of excluding grazing but of managing grazing?

Perhaps with our enthusiasm for new native woods, we should plant other ash woods on limestone outcrops elsewhere?

9. MORRONE BIRKWOOD
NATIONAL NATURE RESERVE, BRAEMAR
Mar Estate, managed by Scottish Natural Heritage
Open – you are asked to keep to the footpaths
(See first photo section)

Drive up the hill out of Braemar, stop in the startlingly ugly car park, pass a couple of incongruous peacocks and a pond full of bread-hungry Mallard, walk up the track and through the deer fence and you are in Morrone, one of the most delectable woods in Scotland.

Barring a few aspen, the trees are all neat, smallish, spreading, widely-spaced birches. If you look closely, you will see that they have all the characteristics of downy birch, *Betula pubescens*, except downiness. They are the subspecies *odorata*. They smell delicious after rain.

What makes Morrone unique is that it is sitting on a rock type very rare in Scotland: a Dalradian calcareous schist with bands of limestone. The consequence, for a subarctic, birch-juniper wood, is an unusually rich and diverse flora, in below the juniper, among the grassy lawns, on the crags and knolls and in the mires and flushes. Diligent botanists have recorded nearly 300 higher plants and as many bryophytes and lichens. On the back of the rich flora is an equally rich insect life. There is nothing like it closer than Norway. The evidence is that what you see now is a direct descendant from the early post-glacial period. It is, in the exact sense of that overused word, irreplaceable.

Morrone has been a National Nature Reserve since 1972. It is a candidate to become a Special Area of Conservation – a European designation. It is managed by SNH under an agreement with Mar Estate, not to be confused with Mar Lodge Estate. The task is to ensure the future of the trees without endangering the special flora. Five years ago something like a third of the 340 ha reserve was enclosed within a deer fence. The regrowth of birch has been spectacular – much of it, I suspect, from regeneration already present but grazed flat. The response was expected because it had been achieved in half a dozen trial enclosures established about 20 years ago which are now, in places, arguably too dense with thicket birch for the health of the juniper struggling underneath. What now? SNH do not have the option of controlling deer numbers overall as at Creag Meagaidh or the NTS at Mar Lodge. The interim answer is that the deer fence will remain for a further ten to fifteen years but it may be necessary to increase grazing within the enclosure by, for example, allowing in some hinds to add to the muzzles of roe, rabbits and hares already there. In practice the management of Upper Deeside is shifting so rapidly that some alternative may become sensible well within this timescale. I am greatly in favour of drawing on the reservoir of energy and skill always present in local communities for monitoring and promoting an intricate, long-term project. Is there scope here for a Friends of Morrone?

10. MOUND ALDERWOOD, SUTHERLAND
Cambusmhor Estate, Mr Abel-Smith
Private but easily visible from the Mound

Compared with other native trees like birch, oak or pine, alder does not get much of a press and yet it is a tree with a deeply interesting past and, at least potentially, a revitalised future if flood plains become more pressing on the consciousness of householders, planners, insurance companies and so forth. Scotland without alder would be ecologically and visually damaged. It is the native tree for wet and very wet places. It is important to say this now because there is an unpleasant disease around known as crown-dieback, which is hovering on the brink of an epidemic. At this stage nobody is certain about the cause or causes. Public concern is required to unlock the resources that the scientists need to study the problem now, before there is a crisis.

If you want to feast your senses on alder there is nowhere better in Britain than the Fleet or Mound Alderwood in Sutherland. After the embankment or Mound, as it is known, was built across the outlet of Loch Fleet in 1816 by Thomas Telford, thus preventing tidal flow, the estuary rapidly filled in with alder and common sallow. Occasional grazing by deer and cattle aside, this remarkable system has gone its own way for near enough two centuries. To enter the area you need permission from the estate, a good balance, a slightly bizarre taste for sploshing about and very reliable gumboots. It is perhaps better to content yourself with the view from the Mound.

People who estimate these things say there are about 1.5 million alder in Scotland. They are everywhere, though they have only been planted in Orkney and Shetland. The pollen record shows a surge in alder about 7,000 years ago which has been used to mark the transition from the dryer Boreal to the wetter Atlantic Period. Donald McVean showed in the 1950s that alder was failing to set good seed in the Highlands above about 300 metres, suggesting that existing alder stands above that limit had been established during a more continental phase of climate in the middle of the nineteenth century.

The wood of alder has been much used in the past, as John Evelyn records, for 'Piles, Pumps, Water pipes, Troughs, Sluces'. Much of Venice rests upon alder poles, as did crannogs. It was the preferred charcoal for gunpowder and the preferred wood for sabots or clogs. I find it difficult to believe that we have reached the end of our interest in using particular woods and prefer to think, or at least hope, that the last half-century or so has been an aberration. Be that as it may, nobody can fail to respond to the vivid blood-red of fresh-cut alder wood. For most people the response is a pleasurable one; in some cultures, however, the red wood is regarded as ominous.

NATIVE TREES

11. SCOTS PINE *PINUS SYLVESTRIS*
BALLOGIE ESTATE, POTARCH BRIDGE, ABERDEENSHIRE
Colonel Nicol
Private but you can get permission from the Estate office

Just about everyone knows of the Caledonian pinewoods. Not everyone, however, knows of the 200-year tradition of growing Scots pine in plantation, though it is not possible to drive through Deeside or Speyside or the Laigh of Moray without becoming conscious of enormous numbers of straight trees growing at careful intervals on ground innocent of almost anything else except sparse heather. They greatly pleased my mother-in-law, a woman for whom 'neatness' earned maximum points. She would have got on well with Queen Victoria, whose insistence on straight telegraph poles laid the way open for a home-grown industry both in east Scotland and at Windsor. It takes a while to grow a pine big enough for the saw bench but the slow-grown timber is excellent. Fresh cut, it smells oddly of strawberries.

The sawmilling industry, and thus the grower of trees, is as subject to trends in the global economy as everyone else: a strong pound, cheap imports from low-wage countries and similar staples of 'econo-speak'. Other industries do not, however, face the nightmare of waking up one morning to find that their supply material, vertical yesterday, is now horizontal. Everyone in these windy islands must expect to experience at least one catastrophic windblow during a lifetime. Recent Scottish

incidents occurred on Boxing Day 1998 in Arran and Ayr; 14–15 January 1968 in Argyll and the Carron Valley by Fintry; and 31 January 1953 in north and particularly north-east Scotland.

During the summers of 1953 and '54 I worked as a cutter for a hastily established timber camp christened Jonesville, on the timber blown down on the Ballogie Estate. The camp was named for the timber merchants who built it, Jones of Larbert. It was a memorable experience enlivened by sharing a bothy with an elderly gentleman who believed in perking up our forester's stove by pouring paraffin in at the top. He had no eyebrows and precious little hair.

In that 1953 gale, Ballogie lost nearly 160 ha of Scots pine, mainly from the 1860 Tomnahay and Baron's Wood. Watchers from Kincardine O'Neil said that great swathes of the trees went over together. The blow was particularly hard on the estate because Ballogie had had nearly 500 ha of trees cut by the Canadian Timber Corps during the Second World War.

Against the odds, one superb pine survived. It is thought to date from 1792 and has borne the name 'Queen of the Firs' at least since Scots pine was known throughout Scotland as the 'Scotch Fir'. The tree was last measured by Jim Paterson in 1994. He made it 128 ft high and 15 ft girth. The size is memorable but even more so is the extraordinarily straight and cylindrical stem running high into the strong crown, and the platy-bark, which has been likened to the shell of a turtle or the skin of an alligator.

12. SESSILE OAK *QUERCUS PETRAEA*
MEADS OF ST JOHN, DARNAWAY ESTATE, NAIRN
The Earl of Moray
Open on foot
(See first photo section)

It is clear from references in the Exchequer Rolls and the Treasurer's Accounts that Darnaway was an important source of oak from the late thirteenth to the early sixteenth century, not least because it was a royal forest. Oak from Darnaway, for example, went into the roof of the cathedral church of Dornoch in 1291 and Randolph's Hall within the estate in 1387.

Looking at Darnaway estate today, however, it is easy to share the view of the 17th Earl of Moray when he wrote in 1928 that only in 'areas very limited in extent are pockets of soil to be found suitable for the production of well-developed Hardwood trees'.

I believe there are three possible reasons for this apparent contradiction.

First, the area growing oak at Darnaway during earlier centuries may have extended further north towards Forres and the sea than that used at present, and thus would have covered the more fertile soils that are now used for agriculture. A telling example of what that would mean for the growth of oak is available for study. It is a half moon of alluvial flat within Darnaway, charmingly called the Meads of St John. Most of the flat is cultivated as farmland but there is a line of 151 oaks along the riverside. They have had virtually unimpeded growth and are all about 14 ft in girth and about 100 ft high. They are unmistakably sessile oaks in form as well as leaf. They were probably planted in the early years of the 9th or 'Planting Earl', 1767–1807. On that basis they would have been something like 60 years old at the time of the devastating Great Moray Floods of August 1829. The 'beautiful vale of St John' is recorded as having 'suffered severely' by Sir Thomas Dick Lauder, who was an eyewitness. The branches of some of the trees may have been broken off by the swirling flood waters and then regrown. This has given the trees the appearance of having been pollarded – an ancient form of tree management.

Second, the location of oak was all important in the long centuries of primitive overland travel. For example, the original roofing timbers for the Great Hall of Stirling Castle, completed in 1503, probably came from Poland, a few hundred miles up the river Vistula. The long journey by water was relatively easy compared to what would have been a laborious overland journey. Wood from Darnaway, situated close to the River Findhorn, would therefore have been transportable relatively easily to Stirling, Leith or other Scottish landfalls.

Third, before the days of power-driven saws, an ideal tree was one that would do the job required if roughly shaped by axe and adze. Medieval craftsmen accepted sapwood, shakes or fissures, even bark, in their structural timbers. The oak timbers used in major buildings at the time did not, therefore, have to be, by present standards, of perfect quality and extra large. Their judgement has been proven sound by the test of time. A contemporary example of this approach is available in the splendid reroofing of the Great Hall of Stirling Castle, which was completed, with careful regard for authenticity, by Historic Scotland in 1994. The roof required about 350 oaks. They were cut from Forest Enterprise woods in Strathyre. The ideal size of tree, according to Archie McConnell who milled the timber, was 16 ft up to about 23 ft in length, and what he described as 'huggable', meaning something you can get your arms around, or about 6 ft in girth or 2 ft in diameter. These are quite small oaks by contemporary standards and thus much easier to find and move.

The traditional connection between Darnaway and important Scottish buildings is being sustained. Three of the finest oaks on the estate have been planked by a Cromarty sawmill, for the new Scottish Parliament at Holyrood.

13. THE KING OF THE WOOD *QUERCUS ROBUR,* JEDBURGH

One field across from the Capon Tree which is signposted, adjacent to the A68 about one mile south of Jedburgh. Park at Hundalee Bridge
Lothian Estates
Open

However long you live, there are no trees more important in your life than those with which you grew up. This truth I agreed, in one of the more bizarre moments of my career, with Frank Bruno, who had been enthralled with the one scruffy tree in his east London street.

I was fortunate. My boyhood centred on a large Victorian garden on the edge of Jedburgh, which contained what seemed like every possible kind of tree. The only species of interest to my friends and I were those we could use, thus, presumably echoing early man. Monkey puzzle branches made the best scimitars. Horse chestnuts yielded enormous numbers of 'cheggies', even in the presence of red squirrels. Ash was the preferred species for catapults and pear for daggers. We made whistles out of rowan and 'blood' out of ripe elderberries. Laurel leaves exploded when thrown on a bonfire. The bast of lime made hallucinogenic 'cigarettes'. Moreover, the territory covered by our gang included the Capon Tree, a renowned, collapsing, 500-year-old oak on the edge of the main road south. What we also knew was that, across one field from the Capon Tree and up the banking, there was a monumental oak called the King of the Wood.

I went to see it again this year. It is even better than I remembered from half a century ago. More or less 20 ft round, with huge basal burrs, a straight, powerful trunk, a few massive, horizontal boughs breaking into knees and crooks and a green, vigorous top without any sign of going back (a forester's term for dying at the extremities). It is unmistakably a pedunculate oak. Conversely and surprisingly, given its form and location, the Capon Tree is a sessile oak.

Over the last decade or so, there has been a gathering interest in what are now deemed 'veteran trees'. A principal driving force has been Ted Green, based at Windsor Great Park. The movement has been formalised into the Ancient Tree Forum. English Nature has recently published a defining text entitled *Veteran Trees: A Guide to Good Management*. Thanks to the energetic Borders Forest Trust and others there is now a rapid spread of this thinking into Scotland. By these well-informed and strongly argued standards, much of the previous management of veteran trees has been, to put it kindly, inappropriate though well intentioned. The King of the Wood has, mercifully, had no

management and needs none. You will probably be able to go and celebrate it anytime over the next 100 years or more.

14. THE KILMALIE ASH *FRAXINUS EXCELSIOR*
KILMALIE OR KIMALLIE, ARGYLL
Burnt down
(See first photo section for another example of a fine ash)

Ash will grow in varying degrees of moisture and lime but will only become impressive on deep, fertile, base-rich soils that are well watered without getting close to water-logging. Since, in the main, such soils are occupied by intensive farming and since many intensive farmers are hostile to field trees, there are fewer big ash trees to be seen today than in nineteenth-century paintings of the Scottish lowlands. So, exceptionally, I have decided to write about an ash tree long departed.

From 1879, Robert Hutchison of Carlowrie, Newliston, published in the *Transactions of the Scottish Arboricultural Society*, accounts and lists of 'Old and Remarkable Trees in Britain'. Eventually he had covered Spanish chestnuts, sycamores, ash trees, oaks, beeches, walnuts, elms, limes and horse chestnuts. He drew on the 1808 *Catalogue of Remarkable Trees* by, in his own words, 'that worthy and quaint old student of nature', Dr Walker, Professor of Natural History at the University of Edinburgh; on correspondence with tree owners and their foresters; and on his own considerable field experience. Here is what he had to say about the Kilmalie Ash.

> Dr Walker and other tree historians have recorded a celebrated ash which stood in the churchyard at Kilmalie, Argyleshire; which is a common position in which to find old ash trees in other parishes in Scotland, whether from any superstition or not in regard to it, has never been ascertained. This Kilmalie ash was long supposed to be the biggest tree in North Britain. It was held in reverence by Lochiel, at whose parish church it stood, and by

his retainers and clansmen, and this fact probably hastened its demolition, for in 1746 it was burnt by the soldiery to the ground. Examined in October 1764, its circumference could then be traced very accurately, and its diameter was found to be in one direction, 17 feet 3 inches, and its cross diameter, 21 feet. Its circumference at the ground, taken before two credible witnesses, was 58 feet. It grew in rich deep soil, about 30 feet above sea level, with a small rivulet running within a few yards of its site. It was described then by one who had known it before its destruction, as not a tall tree, for it divided into three great arms about 8 feet from the ground.

There is a puzzle here and perhaps a solution. Most ash in Scotland do not live much above 200 years and, even on the best sites, do not have time to grow in girth to anything approaching the Kilmalie tree. Fine trees like the one in the Bush Estate outside Roslin may be no more than 12 ft in girth. However, trees that have been cut back live longer and have bigger boles. It would satisfy logic if this ash had been a pollard, and why not, since ash boughs make good fodder, ash timber is light and strong, ideal for agricultural implements and ash was a sacred tree, the life of which should be extended.

There are no other records about the height of the Kilmalie Ash. I doubt if it got anywhere near the 120 ft of the tallest known today, a tree in the warm and fertile Carse of Gowrie.

15. WYCH ELM *ULMUS GLABRA*
BRAHAN, DINGWALL, EASTER ROSS
Mr and Mrs Andrew Matheson
Call at the Estate Office for permission

Somewhere I learnt that James McNab, who followed his father William as Curator of the Royal Botanic Garden Edinburgh (RBGE), their joint reign running from 1810 to 1878, was very interested and active in hybridising elms. His productions were then planted out at Inverleith Park opposite the RBGE and on the Meadows in south Edinburgh. If you look at these elms, especially as the leaves are coming off, you have no difficulty in believing that they are mongrels. My favourite (inside the Garden) is labelled *Ulmus minor x plotii x glabra var. glabra.*

It is not infrequently the case that elms in and around towns are introductions or hybrids. A familiar of the Edinburgh 'treescape', for example, is the unmistakable triangle of the Wheatley elm, so late into leaf that it is occasionally assumed to be dead and always the last to lose its leaves. In a mild winter they may still be there at Christmas. I also remember a large, perfectly formed Huntingdon elm on the eastern edge of Elgin, so placed that the rising winter sun set it in dramatic silhouette for drivers on the A96. I hope it is still there.

Away from towns, any elm is likely to be the wych or Scots elm. Wych, incidentally, according to Geoffrey Grigson comes from the Old English 'wice', from a Germanic base meaning 'pliant' or 'bending'. This was, and could still be, if anyone cared to grow it as such, a valuable timber tree. 'It is,' said the 6th Earl of Haddington, 'both strong, of Fine Colour, and Prettyly Veined, very Little Inferour to the Mohogany and some of the West Indian Timber, so much in Request, for Chests, Chairs, Tables and Cabinets.'

Wych elm is not, as many people hoped at first, resistant to the virulent strain of Dutch Elm Disease which entered Britain from America via Liverpool in 1976. The Scottish summers have, however, proved less helpful to the spread of a disease that has wiped out the elm population further south, though it is returning as sucker regrowth from the roots. Moreover, since the fungal spores are carried from tree to tree by a flying beetle, it is helpful when an elm is isolated as is this splendid tree, on the way down to the river below the house at Brahan. It is dying back but only from old age, which for a wych elm might start at about 250 years. These days, old, stagheaded trees are valued aesthetically and ecologically.

Elms are the subject of an indisputable masterpiece of a British book on trees. It is called simply, *Elm* by R.H. Richens and was first available in 1983.

16. ASPEN *POPULUS TREMULA*, BOAT OF GARTEN
Between the A9 and the B9153 from Carrbridge south
(See first photo section)

For those of us who think of aspen as a particularly highland tree, with some outstations in the south, it is chastening to read about its wide geographical distribution. Clapham, Tutin and Warburg say, 'Europe from Iceland, Scandinavia, Northern Russia, to south Spain, Sicily, Greece and the Caucasus; temperate Asia to Japan, south to Asia Minor; Algeria'. If you throw in the closely related North American *Populus tremuloides*, there is not much left of the northern temperate zone without a trembling poplar.

There is a much-quoted passage about aspen in the *Carmina Gadelica*:

> Clods and stones and other missiles, as well as curses, are hurled at the aspen by the people of Uist because it was used to make the cross on which Christ was crucified.
>
> No crofter or fisherman would use aspen wood for any purpose.

The only poplars referred to in the Bible are thought to be *Populus alba, P. nigra* and *P. euphratica*. All poplars have a family resemblance and the absence of aspen from Israel has not stopped anyone believing what they will about the trembling poplar. It grows copiously in the Western Isles.

Aspen needs a fertile mineral soil, which is one reason why you will often see it by the side of a burn. Another is that waterside cliffs, cleughs and ravines may be refugia from the ever-seeking muzzles of sheep and deer. You need, though, a rock face almost as sheer and unbroken as

Edinburgh Castle before anything is safe from goats. The time to look for aspen is late October to early November when the clean, flaring yellow of its leaves is separable from everything else. Frequently it will be a clump or grove deriving from root suckers. The individual stems are relatively short lived; the clump is, I suppose, theoretically immortal.

Until recently, orthodoxy had it that the production of seed was very rare in Scotland and thus the extension of the species was dependent on vegetative propagation. Then Rick Worrell and others holed orthodoxy below the waterline. It is now clear that aspen does produce seed from time to time, more from some clones than from others, more in some places than in others. At long intervals, after very warm summers like 1995, it can produce spectacularly large quantities. The seed is as light as a dandelion seed and will be blown as far. It has a short natural life and will only germinate and grow if it falls on a suitable substrate, where competition is sparse or absent. This is now a satisfactory explanation of why aspen was so successful in the early post-glacial period.

Not everyone likes aspen any more than they do, or did, in Uist. Here is my favourite, the 6th Earl of Haddington, in characteristic flow, not mincing his words:

> I know of no use they are for, and they run through the whole Ground, spoiling Grass, and every thing that is near them, so that were my Advice taken, they who are so unlucky as to have them, should root them out, as fast as they can, and none should Attempt to poison their Grounds, with so pernicious a weed.

I owe to the observant Graham Tuley, formerly Forestry Commission Native Woodland Advisor in the north, the observation that there are some particularly good aspen between Boat of Garten and Carrbridge.

17. HOLLY *ILEX AQUIFOLIUM*
FIONN LOCH, WESTER ROSS
Paul van Vlissingen, Letterewe Estate
Open

Everyone, once in their lifetime, should look down a high-power microscope at a pollen grain or, preferably, pollen grains. The magnification has to be x400 or x600, or occasionally up to x1500. Some pollen grains can only be identified as to genus – the two British oaks, for example – but many are as plain as a barn door.

When M.J.C. Walker and others declare that holly was once a major constituent of the flora of upland Nairnshire, they are basing their statements on pollen analysis of peat. Their observations are as accurate as the contrasting ones of present-day observers such as Mary McCallum Webster, author of the standard *Flora*, who note that the present distribution of holly in Nairn is 'often planted or bird sown. In woods, by hedges, on cliffs and among rocks on moors.' Here, as elsewhere, holly now seems to be common only where grazing animals have had restricted access.

One such place further north is this island in the Fionn Lochs which runs north of and parallel to Loch Maree in the excellent country of Letterewe. This small wood of hollies seems first to have been described by Donald McVean in 1962.

To find the present distribution across Scotland, you can use the *Atlas of the British Flora*, which shows holly everywhere except Caithness and the Northern Isles. It is more common in the west, except in the protection of woods because, despite the waxy coating, the leaves are vulnerable to cold, dry winters.

For a properly referenced and thorough account of plant lore you can consult Tess Darwin's *The Scots Herbal*. All the facts are here: holly is evergreen, prickly, covered in red berries, capable of surviving more or less indefinitely (if protected from browsing) after being coppiced or cut back or lightly grazed, an excellent firewood, an even-grained, dense, white, carving wood and known to everyone.

In *Flora Britannica* (1996), Richard Mabey compiled not an antiquarian lore of plants but the experiences and attitudes of ordinary contemporaries. He tried to stimulate correspondents from Scotland but was only partially successful. Nonetheless, in the eight pages devoted to holly there is much of interest and relevance to us. There is confirmation that 'its leaves have one of the highest calorific contents of any tree browsed by animals, and are rich in nutrients', that the traditional practice of feeding stock and deer on the leaves continues and that woodmen are superstitious about felling holly as they believe it may bring bad luck. That is the reaction I have encountered in Argyll and in the New Forest, Hampshire.

Holly berries are eaten by many birds and the seeds thus distributed far and wide. It will grow on many soils provided they are not too wet or too acid. It is a useful indicator of grazing pressure, not least in upland Nairn or an island on Fionn Loch.

18. THE ARRAN WHITEBEAMS *SORBUS ARRANENSIS*, ARRAN SERVICE TREE *SORBUS PSEUDOFENNICA* GLEN DIOMHAN, NATIONAL NATURE RESERVE, NORTH ARRAN

Arran Estates
Open

According to the World Wildlife Fund (WWF) there are in the order of 100,000 tree species in the world, of which, in the view of WWF, some 8,000 are under threat of extinction from fire, logging, forest clearance and climate change. They may be wrong in terms of detail but the scale of the problem is not in doubt. West Africa lost about half its tropical forests and Latin America almost a third in the 30 years from 1960 to 1990. Present-day Indonesia does not bear thinking about.

On the endangered list are 11 British tree species. All are members of the genus *Sorbus*, meaning whitebeams and rowans. All are endemic, meaning confined to a particular area. Most grow on limestone, along the coasts of Devon and Somerset, on the banks of the Bristol Avon, in the Wye valley and on the northern escarpments of the Brecon Beacons. The exceptions to the rule of southern location and lime conditions are these two species confined to North Arran, with a particular concentration in Glen Diomhan. (A Gaelic-speaking friend tells me this is pronounced more or less 'jeevan' and means 'idle'.)

It is slightly disingenuous of WWF to add these to the world's endangered species as the pollen record suggests that the Arran whitebeams have never been common. Botanists have known of their existence and importance since at least 1869, the NNR was notified in 1965. Active measures are in place to conserve the population; there are about 500 of each species on Arran.

The explanation for the existence of these *Sorbi* is an odd phenomenon called agamospermy, a mechanism that enables a species to produce viable seed without sexual fertilisation. The offspring are genetically identical to the single parent. I learn from the impeccably accurate Philip Lusby of the RBGE, in his publication *Scottish Wild Plants*, that pollen, usually from the equally native but non-endemic rowan, is a necessary trigger despite the asexuality of the process.

On the basis of their appearance, it is suggested that *S. arranensis* might be a cross between the native rowan and rock whitebeam (*S. rupicola*) and *S. pseudofennica*, a backcross between *S. arranensis* and rowan. They can be studied in the safety of the RBGE or by a longish trek into this steep-sided, sparsely vegetated glen in north-west Arran. When I was there with a friend some years ago we were accompanied almost throughout by an inquisitive golden eagle.

19. THE FORTINGALL YEW *TAXUS BACCATA*
FORTINGALL, GLEN LYON
The Church of Scotland
Open

Mexicans arriving at the Fortingall Yew, billed as the oldest tree in Europe, with the image in their mind of their own oldest tree, El Thule, a Montezuma cypress 140 ft high and a massive 119 ft round, must prepare for a disappointment. The foliage at Fortingall is vigorous enough but it is not more than 20 or 30 ft off the ground and it grows from not more than 10 per cent of the 'low rampart rim' of an original circumference. With the best of intentions and probably wisely, the authorities have not helped public viewing of the shell by enclosing it within high stone walls with the odd aperture. The history of the Fortingall Yew is, however, all that you could wish.

It was first described and illustrated by Thomas Pennant in 1769. He shows small lollipop bushes growing from both sides of the rim but records that Captain Campbell of Glen Lion (sic), as a boy 'rode on the then connecting part'. Jacob Strutt in *Sylva Britannica*, 1826, shows the halves separated and a carriageway through the middle.

It is impossible to date old yews exactly. All are hollow. All have had periods of slower and faster growth, the latter, according to Elwes and Henry, when 'old trees have lost their heads and the stem is covered with young shoots'. In old age, in an important sense, yews do not behave like trees at all but like hazel or bracken or even wood anemone, vegetation which is capable of renewing itself by rooting outwards more or less indefinitely. Where growing conditions appear to be similar, it is tempting to accept that a yew of a given girth is likely to be older than one of a much lesser girth. Pennant measured the base of the Fortingall Yew as 56 ft. Alan Mitchell reckoned that this equated with 40 ft at 5 ft, the standard height for comparisons of girth. The largest girthed yew in Britain today is 34 ft, at Ulcombe Church, Kent. The largest Scottish yew is at Ormiston, approaching 20 ft. Allen Meredith, who knows as much about English yews as anyone, suggests that 31 ft might equate with 3,000 years and 35 ft 6 in. with 5,000 years. Not everyone agrees. All that one can say is that there is a plausible case for the Fortingall Yew being very old.

Earlier botanists accepted that yew is native in Scotland, albeit sparse. Professor Jim Dickson of Glasgow University, after reviewing the classic sites, concludes that at none is the evidence absolutely secure. They are at Bernera on Lismore, Glenure in Appin, Kilmalieu, Kingairloch, Minard Point, Lorne and Inchlonaig in Loch Lomond. For good measure he has looked at the five fossil and archaeological records for yew, with the same result.

Did someone, several years ago, bring a yew from the south and plant it at Fortingall and, if so, why?

20. THE GREAT YEW OF ORMISTON *TAXUS BACCATA* ORMISTON HALL, EAST LOTHIAN
The Ormiston Hall Group
Private but visitors welcome

Sir Thomas Dick Lauder of Relugas on the Findhorn, then of Grange House in south Edinburgh, was not one to hide his light under a bushel. His 1834 edition of Gilpin's *Remarks on Forest Scenery* is so laced with his own opinions and substantial knowledge of trees that you have to turn back several pages to establish what is Sir Thomas and what is the equally well-informed and opinionated William Gilpin. Sir Thomas thought the Great Yew of Ormiston 'one of the finest objects as a vegetable production that Scotland can exhibit'. It was 'throwing out its vast limbs horizontally in all directions, supporting a large and luxuriant head, which now covers an area of ground 58 ft in diameter with a most impenetrable shade'. He measured the trunk at 4 ft as 14 ft 9 in.

Now, nearly 170 years later, the Great Yew remains a huge green tent, as healthily vigorous as ever. Girth has increased at 4 ft to 19 ft 3 in. In his comprehensive and meticulous 1992 survey of Scottish yews – as yet

unpublished – Jim Paterson shows that there are no trees in good health with a larger girth.

I have said already that dating old yew trees accurately has proved to be impossible. It does not help that measurements are often wildly inaccurate and historical records often flawed or even faked. What can

be said about the Ormiston yew is that when John Cockburn sold the
estate to the Earl of Hopetoun in 1747, one of the papers handed over
was a deed 'signed under the Yew Tree'. The deed is missing. The date of
the deed was said to be 1474 but only in the 'recollections of a
Gentleman who saw it'. The tree may therefore be 700 years old, and

could be a good deal older. Whatever the age, it is a remarkable 'vegetable production' guaranteed to excite the most laid-back of grandchildren. Some of mine described it as 'cool'. Given the attention that we pay to Melrose Abbey, say, or the Black Wood of Rannoch, it is odd that there is no appropriate recognition or designation for the Great Yew. How about 'National Heritage Tree'?

It is in doubt whether, as folklore has it, George Wishart ever preached under the Great Yew but it was certainly at Ormiston, on 16 January 1546, that he was seized and sent on his way to martyrdom at St Andrews.

THE RESTORATION OF
NATIVE WOODLAND

21. CARRIFRAN WILDWOOD
OFF THE A708 BETWEEN MOFFAT AND THE GREY
MARE'S TAIL
Borders Forest Trust, Monteviot Nurseries, Ancrum
Open

Carrifran, originally Corriefaine perhaps meaning 'Corrie of the Raven', is a 600 ha glen in the Moffat hills. It is an entire catchment because a central concern of those involved is that they must be able to monitor the effects of their project, without confusion with any other land use.

The fundraisers in the team still look amazed that, from a standing start in 1992, they managed to raise a third of a million pounds to buy the land. They have attracted 600 'founders' and 1,000 other contributors because of their vision, the quality of their enthusiasm and their evident grasp of what they are attempting to do. They have touched a chord. Their vision – no less a word will do – is to restore to this glen the mixed native woodland removed a few thousand years ago and prevented from returning by grazing beasts, domestic and wild.

The 40-strong Wildwood group are friends mainly from around Peebles, drawn together by this shared vision but coming from many different backgrounds relevant to the needs of the project. They are biologists, ecologists, accountants, all sorts; amateurs only in the sense that they have not done this before. The Borders Forest Trust is the umbrella organisation drawing together native woodland initiatives throughout the Borders.

Incidentally, if you want to see a fully realised landscape plan look on the BFT website for a study of the dossier prepared (an integral part of the Environmental Impact Assessment required by the Forestry Commission) as a precondition for grant aid. The Forestry Commission can be justly proud of having pioneered forest landscape planning worldwide and will be gratified to see this arcane skill become an everyday, robust, sensible reality.

The first phase of planting in the lower glen is complete. Seed has been collected from residual trees in the locality, grown in gardens or nurseries, and the new transplants – ash, oak, birch, bird cherry, rowan, hawthorn and so forth – have been planted at random intervals across the hill, leaving ample gaps around the flushes, banks and burns. There are hazards ahead: goats and sheep immediately but later, frost, voles, deer, competition from the rampant, ungrazed grass or one of those unknowns that projects are heir to. It is not luck that you must wish this project, but robust forest management.

In the very long term the intention is to let this new/old woodland take a natural course and succumb to wind or what you will without further human interference. It will be a living, and dying, laboratory, but one of beauty and great interest.

22. GLEN FINGLAS, BRIG O' TURK
The Woodland Trust
Open on foot or mountain bike

I met Kenneth Watkins, founder of the Woodland Trust, in the early 1960s near his home in south Devon. He was then much concerned about the fate of broadleaved woodland in his local area. I imagine that in his old age he would have been astonished at the growth of 'his' Trust. From a start in 1972 it now has over 1,000 sites across Britain covering more than 16,000 ha. He would have been incredulous at his creation acquiring, with the generous support of the Heritage Lottery Fund, over 4,000 ha of glen on the eastern edge of the Trossachs.

Glen Finglas is a collective name embracing Glen Meann, Glen Casaig and Lendrick as well as Glen Finglas proper. If you have ever stood on Ben Ledi, the Trust property is a sizeable chunk of everything you see to the immediate west. Glen Finglas was a royal hunting forest from the earliest times and, because relatively accessible to the Stewart kings, who were madly keen on hunting, pretty actively used and managed. All that came to a halt when James VI and I went south. The area became hugely popular around 1800, under the stimulus of Sir Walter Scott, who described it in *The Lady of the Lake* and his poem *Glenfinlas*. It even became a retreat for John Ruskin.

What makes Glen Finglas unusual and important is the remnant trees, here and there aggregated into somewhat moth-eaten, open woodland. There are reckoned to be 235 ha of trees overall or 6 per cent of the whole area, but it is not the quantity but the distribution which is relevant. What you are looking at is, or would be but for the Trust, the death throes of a landscape which, two centuries ago, was commonplace in upland Scotland. That is a landscape where trees, domestic animals and deer were managed to coexist. Glen Finglas probably survived, as most other glens did not, principally because the owner, the Earl of Moray, was based so far away. The types of trees are what you would expect, as is their concentration along gulleys and burnsides. Of most interest are some very old hazels and alders in Glen Finglas itself, the form of which suggest management as upland wood pasture. The crucial point is that they are more numerous than usual and perhaps enough to provide a seed source for much of the wished-for regeneration. Given, of course, that deer can be adequatcly controlled.

The Woodland Trust has commissioned a lot of specialist surveys and advice before compiling a 'management plan for the first 25 years'. In a nutshell, the aim is to establish woodland cover on some three-quarters of the 4,000 ha over a period of 30 or 40 years. The areas innocent of existing trees must, perforce, be planted – much of Lendrick has already been completed – but wherever practicable the Trust wish to proceed by natural regeneration. The vision is simple and ambitious: to create a land use where trees, domestic stock, deer and people coexist in a relationship appropriate to our times.

23. CREAG MEAGAIDH
NATIONAL NATURE RESERVE, GLEN SPEAN
Scottish Natural Heritage
Open
(See first photo section)

Until 1983, those people who were aware of Creag Meagaidh knew it for the towering cliffs of Coire Ardair, which offer some of the best winter climbing in Scotland, or as the third and highest of a round of tops (Carn Liath and Stob Poite Coire Ardair being the others) which, given reasonable weather, make a deeply satisfying day in the hills, especially if you can arrange to come off by the Moy Burn.

In 1983 Loch Laggan Estates sold the deer forests of Moy and Aberarder to Fountain Forestry. What happened next became a watershed in the land-use debate in Scotland and has been written up by Donald Mackay, who was a Scottish Office insider at the time. You will not agree with everything that he says but his book should be compulsory reading for anyone trying to understand that pivotal decade. In brief, after a prolonged and highly charged debate, Fountain Forestry sold what is near enough 4,000 ha to the Nature Conservancy Council, now Scottish Natural Heritage, in 1985. They had bought the land for £300,000 and sold it for £431,000.

In 1977, Creag Meagaidh was classified by Derek Ratcliffe as 'Grade 2 upland grassland and heath' and comprised 1.9 per cent of the total in that category identified for conservation in the Western Highlands. The land, now owned by the SNH, became a National Nature Reserve in 1986.

The central objective on this new reserve was 'to encourage

regeneration and extension of native forests and boreal scrub' with minimum interference, particularly fencing. From the outset there was a determination to reduce the deer and sheep numbers to the point where regeneration would begin to appear and flourish. There was no preoccupation with numbers, nor is there now – the test is, just as a farmer's test is, the condition of the sward or herbage. The count and the cull of red deer, for each of the 11 years from 1985 to 1996 are set out in Paul Ramsay's book on Creag Meagaidh, written for SNH, *Revival of the Land*. The latest count was 86. The first was 1,000. The highest annual removal of stags, hinds and calves culled or live captured was 371. The latest was 60.

The appearance of young trees, predominantly downy birch but also rowan, willow and others has been impressive. Dick Balharry, formerly of SNH, who was deeply involved in the philosophy and the practice, is well content. So are the neighbouring deer forests of Tulloch, Glenshero, Braeroy and Ardverikie. There has been no 'vacuum' effect of drawing adjacent deer onto Creag Meagaidh, as had been feared. After 14 years some 600 ha of the reserve fulfil the criteria that, if this were private land, would attract grant aid for natural regeneration from the Forestry Commission.

24. CASHEL OR CAISIL
BETWEEN BALMAHA AND ROWARDENNAN
Royal Scottish Forestry Society Forest Trust Co.
Open

Until 1996 Cashel was a hill farm owned by Jock Maxwell, except for an area either side of the bisecting burn which he had sold earlier for plantation forestry. In that year he sold 1,238 ha to the Royal Scottish Forestry Society (RSFS) or, more precisely, the RSFS Forest Trust, a charitable company limited by guarantee. Board members are drawn from the RSFS. The project manager was Felix Karthaus.

The purchase price of £870,000 came from the Millennium Forest for Scotland Trust (MFST). With this purchase, the first in its 150-year history, the RSFS have bought themselves into the complex ownership of the woods on the east side of Loch Lomond, now swept up into a National Park. Other owners include Forest Enterprise, the National Trust for Scotland, the RSPB and, not very far away at Glen Finglas, the Woodland Trust.

'The vision for Cashel,' to quote the RSFS brochure, 'is to recreate a near-natural sequence of native woodland types, ranging from oakwood near the loch shore, through pine-birch wood on the slope, to open ground sub-montane scrub on the highest ground.' The 'recipe book' for what to plant is *Forestry Commission Bulletin* 112, 'Creating New Native Woodlands'. It draws on the work and publications of John Rodwell of Lancaster University. The highly experienced, highly practical Brian Brookes, once warden of Kindrogan Field Studies Centre, was employed to draw up an ecological map based on the National Vegetation Classification (NVC). The planting pattern follows from that. For an older generation it is reminiscent of M.L. Anderson's *Selection of Tree Species*.

The RSFS set themselves the target of establishing trees on 38 per cent of the site by the year 2000 and have succeeded. They have done so by enclosing all establishment areas with deer fencing, by use of a machine called the Maclarty mounder, by planting container-grown trees from mainly locally collected seed and by using phosphate as deemed necessary. The success of this approach in terms of rocketing tree growth is plain to see. Not everyone thinks it is the most appropriate approach. You will not find a better rehearsal of the debate – planting versus natural regeneration – than in Issue 23, Spring 2000, *Reforesting Scotland*. It is a short, quiet, masterly summary by the Forestry Commission's Native Woodland Advisor for Scotland, the admirably well-informed Peter Quelch.

What is not in dispute is the involvement of an encouraging mix of people in the project: local and not so local, old and, particularly, young.

25. NEW NATIVE PINEWOODS

In 1988 the Forestry Commission announced that 'the higher, or broadleaves rate of grant would apply to natural regeneration and planting in the native pinewoods identified by H.M. Steven and A.C. Carlisle in their book *The Native Pinewoods of Scotland*, together with additional areas which are agreed as suitable for encouraging the extension of native pinewoods'.

I chaired the working group set up to compile detailed guidelines for the scheme. The members were, bless them: Alan Mowle, NCC; Russel Turner, Countryside Commission for Scotland; Mike Abraham, Timber Growers UK; Ian Bainbridge, RSPB; and, as invaluable Forestry Commission secretary to the group, Graham Gill. We had 14 meetings, each lasting several hours. It was a deeply interesting, occasionally frustrating, ultimately very rewarding experience. Rereading the November 1989 booklet brings it all back. Imagine, for example, the hours required to arrive at this paragraph:

> It is desirable to avoid disturbance of the soil profile. There is a preference, therefore, for establishment without mechanical cultivation. Where some form of cultivation is essential to achieve areas of successful establishment, scarifying, particularly patch scarifying, will be the strongly preferred method. When it is accepted that shallow ploughing, mounding or tining is required, the specification will be as light, irregular and intermittent as practicable.

The latest figure that I have for newly established native pinewoods is 13,700 ha. Compare this with the latest figure for existing native pinewoods of 17,882 ha. The schemes are pretty evenly divided across what is generally agreed as the former area of Scots pine-dominated, pine-birch forest.

One of the earliest, perhaps the largest, to take up the scheme was the

Atholl Estate. Fortunately, while it was all fresh in mind, Chris Langton, who was then Woods Manager at Atholl, gave a paper to the 1994 Pinewood conference in Inverness, 'Our Pinewood Heritage', based on his experience of five schemes totalling about 2,500 ha. I can do no better than quote a number of his forthright comments:

> Good management and close supervision of work carried out by highly competent and technically well-qualified contractors and staff has reduced costs . . . the harsh reality of it is that on these high wild areas where, as has occurred each winter so far, long sections of deer fence can be snow-covered, the requirement is simply to kill every deer, rabbit and hare possible within the fence . . .
>
> There is tremendous cooperation and goodwill generally between walkers and estate staff . . . What do you do with a capercailzie or black grouse which insists on attempting to eat its designer-built future? . . .
>
> Having compiled six environmental assessments . . . I now thoroughly approve of them!

What will posterity think of our collective efforts? Nothing that we can guess.

26. CREE VALLEY COMMUNITY WOODLANDS NEWTON STEWART
Various owners – *see text*
Open

Will the Millennium Forest for Scotland Trust have been the most imaginative and enduring memorial to that odd moment in our collective history? Time, as ever, will be the arbiter but, looking through the project list, the MFST has clearly stimulated or responded to an impressive array of people across the country. There are 78 projects on the list that I have. In all cases the MFST contribution cannot be more than half the funding. The contributions range from £4,900 to Tomnacross Primary School at Kiltarlity, to £870,000 for the RSFS at Cashel, Loch Lomond. In round figures, the MFST will have disbursed a total of £8.5 million by the end of the enterprise in 2001: £1.5 million where the contribution in each case is more than £500,000; £5 million where the contribution is between £500,000 and £100,000; and £2 million on the 53 smaller projects.

I liked the look of the Cree Valley project on paper and I liked it even better when I saw it, in the company of the energetic Dr Peter Hopkins, the full-time project coordinator. This is the description of the intent:

> Cree Valley Community Woodlands Trust is a charitable organisation which aims to create a native broadleaved woodland in the River Cree catchment through a partnership with landowners, public agencies and the local community. There are important but fragmented areas of oakwood along the Cree including three SSSIs though these are hemmed in by conifer plantations. The project will extend and link up these oakwoods at 10 sites from above Loch Trool to Newton Stewart (some 14 miles).

The sites are owned by Forest Enterprise, the RSPB, the local authority and private landowners. They are all entering 25-year agreements with Cree Valley Community Woodlands Trust. Of the 550 ha in the project, some 42 per cent is Forest Enterprise land and 49 per cent is RSPB. I particularly like the fact that the state forest service and a major charity are prepared to cede a little of their sovereignty towards a common goal and I am impressed that the commitment is for 25 years. I admire the vision of looking at the valley as a whole and hope that the project will expand to include more non-woodland along the river. I like the bustle of activity and the determination to keep everyone informed.

This is a place to visit in ten years or twenty, remembering that, like all acts of creation, it only happened because someone, or in this case a group of people, wanted it to happen and set about making it happen.

27. KIRKTON FARM, CRIANLARICH
Part of the Scottish Agricultural College Hill and Mountain
    Research Centre, Crianlarich
Open to anyone walking the hill. Occasional official open days or
    on application

A visit to Kirkton Farm in Strathfillan should be on the curriculum vitae of everyone interested in or concerned for the future of the 1,600 hill farms in Scotland.

For as long as anyone alive can remember, domestic stock and trees have, with rare exceptions, been managed separately. Those who look after farm animals and trees in Scotland have been segregated by education, training, employment, union affiliation, membership of professional bodies and government structure, to say nothing of matrimony.

It did not have to be like this. It was not always like this. This is not the way in backwoods Spain or France or Poland or Scandinavia, although, to speak truthfully, traditional systems in these parts of Europe are breaking down. What is being proposed by the Scottish Agricultural College (SAC) is that we reinvent or rather rethink for our own period and purposes, an integration of upland stock rearing and trees. We could show Europe a way forward in the process.

Like the SAC, we need to go back to the much derided but essential basics. Anybody who has found shelter in a wood from an exposed hill on a wild day knows the instant relief, the return of body heat, especially if the wood is not too open, if the lower exterior branches, or skirts, have been retained. Given half a chance, that is where the beasts are also to be found. I have a vivid memory of a disconsolate European bison in a wildlife park in Wales, backed into a thick thorn bush during a torrential storm.

Conversely, there is no doubt that animals eat trees, though, goats apart, not often out of choice. I remember Dartmoor during the terrible winter of 1963–64 when desperate sheep ate the tops of the high elevation oaks in Wistman's Wood, standing on five metres of packed snow. If you have any doubts about the benefits of shelter remember that Palaeolithic red deer living in woodland were more than twice the body weight of their open country descendants.

Future integration must mean not the casual, ultimately destructive exploitation of remnant birchwoods but intelligent, managed integration, variable to animal, season, soil-type and tree species. Within the spectrum most interest will attach to the management of hill sheep in fairly dense and uniform birchwoods on better-than-average soils and in summer. This is what SAC are, or at least will be, exploring, when the trees are big enough. On the 850 ha hirsel of Kirkton Glen, they have planted 250 ha of predominantly birchwood in order, eventually, to make comparison with the 'control' hirsel alongside.

In the meantime, in a parallel project, the SAC are looking at a range of actual woodland grazings and shelters across Scotland. What they find will be communicated urgently to an industry that has taken too many hard knocks.

28. HOY, ORKNEY
See text

Throughout Orkney and on Hoy in particular, there is a mix of professionalism, self-help and group sharing in the pursuit of native woodland restoration that I find admirable.

As an example of co-operation, look at the *Orkney Native Tree Conservation Strategy* prepared for the Orkney Native Tree Group in 1995 by Jenny Taylor. Presented here, in a doggedly unpretentious format, is the present state of knowledge about the extent (tiny), condition (vulnerable), needs (comprehensive) and prospects (better than at any time for 100 years or more) of native trees on the islands.

It is not as though trees will not grow in Orkney. Introduced species like sycamore or Swedish whitebeam get on fine, as did the native tree flora until something like 4,700 years ago. At that point there is a sharp decline in tree pollen in the peat deposits examined. Nobody is sure whether this was due to a climate change or Neolithic farmers or, probably, both. A factor in preventing the return of trees was the development of blanket peat but that was not until some 1,800 years ago. Thereafter, a principal factor seems to have been disinterest, which is odd given the inestimable value of shelter on a windy island. As Jo Grimond wrote once, 'Beware flying Nissen huts.'

It is a shock to realise that there are only three native tree species on Orkney: downy birch, rowan and aspen, plus many botanically confusing shrubby willows and three hazel bushes. Present-day juniper is mainly prostrate but, given shelter and extent, it may grow upright as at Morrone Birkwood, Braemar or in Iceland. Apart from lots of willows and an occasional aspen there are very few native trees outside Hoy.

The cooperation between agencies, organisations and individuals is impressive. The RSPB owns the largest natural woodland at Berriedale on Hoy and it is creating another at Durkadale. The Farming and Wildlife Advisory Group is active, as is the Orkney Island Council and members of the Orkney Field Club. Money and support comes from SNH, the Forestry Commission, MFST and the Orkney Island Council.

A huge cast seems to be involved in learning how to do what needs to be done and doing it. There is a desire for natural regeneration but a preparedness, if necessary, to collect and grow seed or suckers or cuttings or whatever will conserve the genetic inheritance of these isolated populations. The Orkney Native Tree Project has planted 20 ha of native woodland throughout the islands. Many of the plants were raised in small local nurseries that came into being as a result of the project. Best of all is that Kirkwall Grammar School is developing a native tree nursery.

The project is drawing on the experience of Dr Erica Benson of the University of Abertay Dundee, to develop micropropagation techniques for reproducing the three hazel trees.

TRADITIONAL ESTATES

29. BALMORAL CASTLE, CRATHIE, DEESIDE
Her Majesty the Queen
Opening hours, during the summer

For well-researched reasons, mainly to do with climatic match, trees and particularly conifers from the north-west of America and the west of Canada grow very well in Scotland. The best known, because most planted, is the streetwise Sitka spruce. There are another five which grow as well or nearly as well but are a bit more fussy about the site. All were introduced between 1826 and 1853 by collectors sent to the Pacific coast by nurserymen or landowners specifically to find new plants and to send home seed. It is interesting to see the sequence, which looks like this:

    1826 Douglas fir – David Douglas
    1830 Noble fir – David Douglas
    1831 Grand fir – David Douglas
    1832 Sitka spruce – David Douglas
    1852 Western hemlock – John Jeffries
    1853 Western red cedar – William Lobb

You can see excellent examples of all these species everywhere in highland Scotland, particularly in Perthshire, Inverness, Easter Ross and Argyll. There are several arboreta and policy woods where you can see all together. I can't think of any location where they are better presented than at either side of the main drive into Balmoral Castle. There are several reasons for this. First, the trees are widely spaced, so that you can get a good look at them individually. Second, there have been waves of planting: the originals, now some 170 years old, are interspersed with others 70 years and younger. Third, there appears to have been a fairly ruthless policy of removing trees as they became dilapidated. Fourth, the grass is cut short so that you can wander among the trees without getting your feet too wet. Finally, there is a good system of labelling, meaning that you always know what you are looking at. The upper storey of the oldest trees is well over 100 ft high.

I have passed the gates of Balmoral often before. This summer was my first visit. I was impressed not only with the drive but by the riverside trees and the wide sweep of views across the broad lawns. The head gardener was also enjoying the space, having recently arrived from gardening at Bristol Zoo.

30. BLAIRQUHAN ESTATE
STRAITON, MAYBOLE, AYRSHIRE
Mr James Hunter Blair
Opening hours mid-July to mid-August, or by written
   appointment

What Blairquhan has is less common than it used to be: an 800 ha estate in which all the trees continue to be managed with conspicuous care and knowledge. We were taken there as forestry students in the late 1950s to see good private estate forestry practice and, particularly, a variety of European larch from the Tatra Mountains in Poland that was causing excitement. Students could be taken there today with equal benefit. As soon as you enter the drive you know that you are in good hands, confirmed by the parkland trees and the inner core of more fancy specimens around the William Burn castle and the walled garden.

The present laird has established a neatly signed and documented

tree-trail, pointing out the more common species in the pinetum, not least a high-pruned pedunculate oak and a fine fern-leaved beech. Tree number one is the Dool Tree, a sycamore or, in Scots, a great plane, of uncertain age with the unhappy history of having been used as a gallows. The tree is hollow from toe to tip and if you thump it, it makes a most odd sound, unlike any other that I know. The laird may not approve of your thumping his tree, however, any more than do the resident jackdaws.

Despite its age and condition, when the tree is pollarded every few years, the new shoots are as vigorous as you could wish. Such a response must encourage similar management of other elderly trees.

So, go to Blairquhan if you want to see forestry skills applied across the whole spectrum from ornament to profit, or ideally the two combined. If you want particular trees on which to feast your eyes try the Roble beech, *Nothofagus obliqua,* on the slope at the back of the walled garden, or the very fine Western hemlocks on the long drive beside the River Girvan. James Boswell was here in January 1783. 'I was much pleased,' he wrote, 'with my ride and the ancient house and large plane and ash trees at this place delighted my ancient baron soul.'

31. CAWDOR CASTLE, BY NAIRN
The Countess of Cawdor
Opening hours

The handling of the trees at Cawdor is close to exemplary. From the environs of the castle through the park and policy woods to the productive plantations there is a seamless transition from the predominantly beautiful to the predominantly useful, but the useful are not unbeautiful and the beautiful may be very valuable. This balance has been achieved under generations of Cawdors, their factors, foresters and advisors, which is some going, given the political, social and economic upheavals over the centuries.

The legacy of the eighteenth century is still plain to see. So is the

work of the last several decades. I remember the expertise of the kilted laird when, as forestry students, we spent six weeks at Cawdor in the 1950s. (He is said to have sacked the entire forestry squad after breakfast and reinstated them before lunch.) His son, Hugh Cawdor, put the estate on a modern footing, which is being sustained by his widow, the Countess. At the back of recent tree planting it is not difficult to discern 'the Knowledge', as per London cabbies, of Jim Paterson who works at Cawdor and who knows more about the specimen trees of Scotland than anyone living – particularly the oaks, yews and pines.

Here are a few examples. At the entrance to the Castle, beyond the 1713 limes and more or less replacing a famous 200-year-old walnut, is a chestnut-leaved oak, growing well, which you won't see at many places outside Kew. The spruce in the field is a Sargent spruce, an elegant and interesting tree that is rare even in specialist arboreta. The birch by the burn is the unusual but highly appropriate river birch from North America. The oak by the car park is a Hungarian oak, which you plant with confidence if you know its admirable track record in Scotland. Most interestingly of all is the newish avenue of limes in substantial cages. These are Oliver's limes, introduced from China in 1900. It may well be the only avenue of this interesting and beautiful lime in the western world. None of these are rarities for rarities' sake. They are rarities only because few people have had 'the Knowledge' and imagination to plant them.

In the gorge below the Castle, among the Victorian conifers, are Dawn redwood and Nyman's eucryphia. Further on are several hundred big, straight, planted Scots pine, which are, taken together, the finest big sticks of pine timber left in Scotland. They date from 1790. Many went from here to refit the House of Lords. The larches in the Big Wood are younger but as good. I remember in 1957 watching the felling of one larch destined for the boatyard at Buckie – 200 hoppus feet at 10 shillings a foot. Larches for boat building, known as boatskin larch, must be straight and without big knots.

Finally we come to the Big Wood itself, which has been a famous source of oak since at least the fifteenth century. It is now as outstanding for the lichens growing on the trees as for the trees themselves. They are mostly pedunculate oaks planted about 200 years ago. Since deer numbers were reduced, seedling oak are beginning to appear, much to the satisfaction of Cawdor and of SNH, who have designated the Big Wood as a Site of Special Scientific Interest.

SOME CLASSIC SITES OF
PLANTATION FORESTRY

32. CORROUR
LOCH OSSIAN, INVERNESS-SHIRE
Professor Joseph Koerner
Private but visible from the hills all around

Generations of Edinburgh University forestry students spent a week or so at Corrour before the autumn term. The only public way in, then as now, is via Corrour Station, which is on the Glasgow–Fort William line between Rannoch and Tulloch. We took over the youth hostel at the southern end of Loch Ossian and got the use of the estate boat to take ourselves the three miles up the loch to the big house and the experimental plantations established round about it by Sir John Stirling-Maxwell of Pollok.

Sir John wrote up his experiments in a privately printed memoir, *Loch Ossian Plantations 1913*. He revised, extended and reprinted the memoir in 1929, increasing the print run from 100 to 150 copies. He was about to become Chairman of the Forestry Commissioners (1929–32), having been a Commissioner since their inception in 1919 under the chairmanship of Simon, Lord Lovat. The Scottish bias was no accident.

The memoirs are excellent pacy reading. In point of personal knowledge, drive, excitement and honesty they are, to my mind, in the distinguished class of William Boutcher, the 6th Earl of Haddington and Sir Thomas Dick Lauder. The opening of the 1913 memoir is characteristic:

These plantations, intended to improve the landscape and afford shelter for deer, were begun twenty years ago without much consideration. They all lie above the 1,250 feet contour. The soil is poor and for the most part covered with peat . . . since 1902 a lot of experimental work has been put into them . . . especially since we discovered that foresters in Belgium were engaged in a similar undertaking.

Sir John exchanged information, ideas, seeds and plants with a huge cast list. It included not only innumerable landowners in Scotland but Dr Augustine Henry at Kew, the Arnold Arboretum in Boston, contacts in Canada and, increasingly, the research officers of the embryonic Forestry Commission, particularly Mark L. Anderson, who, when he became Professor of Forestry at Edinburgh, insisted that students understand the messages from Corrour.

Here are a few quotations from the 1929 memoir which illustrate how far Sir John had advanced towards what became truisms:

No ground was enclosed that had any value for pasture, and scarcely an acre . . . has not needed some preparation before planting. The earlier planting was done chiefly with Scots pine . . . But we have had to give it up. Of all the trees we have tried this [Sitka spruce] promises the best return. We have in recent years only used seed [of Sitka spruce] from Queen Charlotte Islands. [This became the preferred origin of Sitka spruce for the Forestry Commission.]

33. CULBIN FOREST, MORAY AND NAIRN
Forest Enterprise
Open on foot
(See first photo section)

As every schoolchild knows, or used to know, the fertile Barony of Culbin was overwhelmed by a great storm in 1694 because the laird let his enthusiasm for playing cards run over from Saturday night into the Sabbath. Too late, you will recall, he discovered that his playing partner was the Devil. For long afterwards, we were told, the vagaries of the sand blowing about would uncover the chimneys of the big house and anyone calling down the lum received an answer.

One of the more remarkable moments of my decade as Forest Officer, Moray, was lying behind a bush in Culbin Forest in the company of Sir Roger Bannister, watching the World Orienteering Championships. That did not advance my acquaintance with the great man because we were sworn to silence, but you can't have everything. The orienteers liked Culbin because it was large and apparently featureless except for the roads and rides laid out in a gridiron pattern. They found it deficient in their category of 'fight', meaning thick vegetation that really hinders running. Throughout half the forest there may not appear to be much beneath the pines except mosses, lichens and a special furry heather, but the interlocking ecosystems are surprisingly and hearteningly rich, developing many of the characteristics of more ancient pinewoods, especially among the fungi, mosses and lichens.

Before the Forestry Commission acquired Culbin in the early 1920s, there had been a good deal of planting by the estates of Kincorth, Moy, Dalvey and Brodie but only on the areas which were stable. Most notable was that done by Major Chadwick because his house of Binsness was closest to the mobile sands and he used Corsican as well as Scots pine. As the trees grew the sand rolled in. Some of his 1906 trees are still there, with roots 10 ft or more below the surface of the ground.

The Forestry Commission did not tackle the mobile sands until after the Second World War. I would recommend reading the 1947 booklet about their efforts. It is a small classic not only for the vivid text and the evocative photographs but, subliminally, for the contemporary mood as 'the foresters struggled to subdue the turbulent sands'. Initially the planting of marram grass was tried but this was soon abandoned for thatching with pine branches cut from the older trees or birch or broom or anything else that came to hand. Much of the planting was done with Corsican pine, which has grown well, so long as there is a supply of nitrogen. This may seem a little surprising for a Mediterranean tree. The Laigh of Moray, though, is as dry and warm as anywhere in Scotland during the growing season. Two years out of three you can ripen sweetcorn in an Elgin garden.

The numerous Capercaillie of my day have, alas, gone but there are few places I would rather be for the sense of an open pinewood with the sea never far away and always the chance of a Crested Tit, a Crossbill, a Goshawk or an Osprey fishing in Findhorn Bay.

34. FINDLAY'S SEAT
TEINDLAND FOREST, MORAY
Forest Enterprise
Open on foot

This is James Donaldson reporting on the Laigh of Moray in 1794:

> Perhaps no country of so wide an extent in Scotland, afforded so much the means of establishment by ornamental plantations. The Earl of Fife . . . displayed the superiority of his taste in selecting and planting such uncultivated rising grounds, as he judged would contribute most to this effect . . . to so great an extent is this mode of improvement now carried on, that, it is possible, the whole of the grounds inaccessible to the plough, in the low lands of Moray will soon be covered with all the different species of forest trees.

Between Rothes and Lhanbryde, 530 ha of what became Teindland Forest, one of the earliest acquisitions of the Forestry Commission in 1922, had been so planted in the early decades of the eighteenth century. The trees were mainly Scots pine. On the freely draining soils from the mid-slopes downwards they grew modestly well and were all felled during the First World War or just after. On the top of the hill, however, around Findlay's Seat, the trees got stuck – and there are bushes 100 years old, no higher than your waist. This was the challenge for the Forestry Commission's Research Branch in 1925. If they could find economic means of getting trees to grow on Findlay's Seat, it would unlock some 36,000 ha of similar upland heaths in Forestry Commission forests in eastern Scotland and northern England. They succeeded.

When John Zehetmayr was given the task of writing the 'Afforestation of Upland Heaths' in 1960, he was drawing on, as he wrote, 'an abundance of experimental data such as perhaps never before had been available to a forester'. Much of it was drawn from Findlay's Seat.

The soil at Findlay's Seat, a consequence of geology, glaciation, climate, and land use over millennia is, or rather was, a 'peaty gley podsol, with hard pan over boulder till'. You don't need to be a gardener for that to send a shiver down the spine. Thirty-five years of research demonstrated in a sentence that: 'Every increase in soil disturbance by increased coverage, depth and repetition increases growth.' In due course, the tractor horsepower capable of pulling the type of plough that would make a fundamental, irreversible change became available.

The numbers of black grouse in Scotland are currently at a low ebb. It is therefore bittersweet to recall that, apart from fire, until the numbers fell around 1925, they were the principal cause of damage to young pine. Even in my time I recall research colleagues bemoaning that their experimental areas were chosen by black grouse as preferred lekking sites, confusing the experimental results in the process.

Findlay's Seat is for me, however, where I met the biggest wildcat of my life, sauntering past on a sunny morning. It was swinging its ringed tail without an apparent care in the world.

35. THE LON MOR
INCHNACARDOCH, FORT AUGUSTUS
Forest Enterprise
Open

When the infant Forestry Commission was getting into its stride, there was already a body of knowledge about how to grow trees on the better end of the soils available for forestry in Scotland: the brown earths, podsols and deeper gleys. Pioneering work at Corrour, Durris and Inverliever suggested that it was also possible to grow trees on the vast areas of peat not required for agriculture, but the method of doing so was not clear. What was needed and needed urgently was authentic research. Over the next three decades this work came under the aegis of some of the giants of Scottish plantation forestry – H.M. Steven, M.L. Anderson, James Macdonald and J.A.B. Macdonald among them. Experimental sites were chosen at Borgie, Achnashellach, Glenrigh and Newcastleton but the first and the best known was an area of Inchnacardoch Forest in the Great Glen called the Lon Mor, meaning, from the Gaelic, 'the big waste'.

The Lon Mor was selected by Steven while directing research in the period 1921–25; the first experiments were laid down by Anderson in 1925. They became, in due course, the Professors of Forestry at Aberdeen and Edinburgh respectively. I sat between them once at a student forestry dinner. It became an early exercise in the business of diplomacy.

There are many different types of peat across Scotland, many variations in climate east to west as well as up and down the hill, different methods of ground preparation, different fertiliser regimes and above all, different species. It has taken more than half a century of research to unravel and understand most of the combinations. It is extraordinary how, from the outset, Anderson tumbled to the near necessity for phosphate and the advantages of planting so as to get the roots to lie between the ground surface and an upturned turf.

If you need to know about forestry on these universally common sites across Scotland, get out the half-century old, 1954 *Forestry Commission Bulletin* 22 or, better still, get one of the present research foresters to take you on an historical trip through the Lon Mor.

36. GLENTRESS FOREST, BY PEEBLES
Owned and managed by Forest Enterprise; Management Prescriptions, Edinburgh University
Open

There is a case for saying that the most interesting 120 ha in Scottish forestry are those on the front face of Glentress Forest in the Tweed valley just below Peebles. It is high time that the two parties involved, Forest Enterprise and the University of Edinburgh, started claiming public credit for a joint venture sustained over half a century. They have been reticent for too long. There is no forester in Scotland who does not know what you mean by Glentress but scarcely anyone else is aware of the achievements that have been made there.

This experimental area was established in 1952 by a gentleman's agreement between the then Professor of Forestry at Edinburgh, Mark L. Anderson, and the Forestry Commission's then Director for Scotland, Sir Henry Beresford-Peirse. The agreement was that the Commission would continue to own and manage these 120 ha but that the management regime would be prescribed by the University. Anderson believed that mixed, irregular, uneven-aged forests such as the beech-spruce-silver fir forests of the Swiss Jura could have advantages over even-aged forests, where different age classes are separated into distinct areas, in terms of reducing windblow, increasing overall yield and increasing the ratio of sawlogs to less valuable products.

These ideas have often been discussed and tried out from time to time at, for example, Drumlanrig, Corrour, Cawdor, Craigvinean, Faskally and The Hermitage, but Glentress is the only substantial, sustained exploration. There have been manifold problems to identify and overcome – the essence of any experiment – and the project only got into full stride within the last two or three decades. Now there is an admirably confident air that everyone involved knows what to do.

If you want to understand the heart of the argument, obtain from the Forestry Commission their short, neat, objective analysis of 1999 entitled *What is Continuous Cover Forestry?* For good reasons concerning the oceanic climate of Scotland, the soils to which forestry has been largely confined, the principal tree species in use and economic pressures, almost all the forests are currently managed on a system of clear felling, albeit in smaller patches than formerly. Now that the system is informed and underpinned by a tough, practical, professional approach to landscape appraisal and prescription (incidentally the best in the world), it is an efficient, robust and acceptable approach to the majority of the upland forest. Where non-market-place benefits are paramount, continuous cover has great appeal. Even in the windy uplands as much as a quarter of the forest might be so managed. In the lowlands the scope is commensurately larger.

Go to Glentress to see the argument and the possible outcomes in practice. Remember that what you are looking at is not as yet continuous cover forestry, but the long-term transition from one system to another.

COMMUNITY WOODLANDS

37. ABRIACHAN FOREST TRUST, INVERNESS-SHIRE
Abriachan Forest Trust
Open
(See first photo section)

Abriachan is on the west side of Loch Ness. Two-thirds of the way south from Inverness to Drumnadrochit, you take a steep minor road up the hill until you are on the hanging valley under the minor peak of Carn na Leitre at 435 m. Here you can find Loch Laide, which the local poet, Ken Steven, describes as 'a fox's eye'. You will learn a good deal about the place, past and present, from a recent book entitled *Abriachan* by Katharine Stewart, who also lives locally. There are something like 50 households at Abriachan, mostly separated from each other by some distance as a consequence of a crofting past. Most people, perforce, work away from home, many in Inverness or beyond.

What has drawn Abriachan to national attention was the decision of the community to enter negotiations with Forest Enterprise to purchase plantations when they were put on the market in late 1995. Eventually the deal made was the purchase of the 534 ha closest to Abriachan, for £152,000. They are, for the most part, very ordinary plantations of lodgepole pine about 15 years old, but that is not the point. The members of the community have not so much bought forest, as the right to determine and control the future of the land which they see from their windows and which will be in the lifelong memory of their children. Forest Enterprise have been cooperative neighbours, particularly as regards unconstrained access, but management decisions were previously taken in Inverness or further afield. The community, now empowered, while not averse to some timber cutting for its value to the local economy, want to see the conservation or replacement of the plantations with mainly native woodland.

It is a mould-breaking example, though it ought not to be, given the centuries of experience with communal woods in Switzerland, for example, or the Jura. It runs in parallel with the crofters of Assynt and the residents in Eigg. The publicity was very well timed in the run-up to the 1997 election, with Michael Forsyth, as Secretary of State for Scotland, sympathetic to such endeavours. It also struck a chord with the incoming Scottish Executive, who, on 8 July 1999, chose to launch their White Paper on Land Reform at Abriachan. It is the largest community-owned forest in Britain.

In the manner of all pioneers, the Abriachan Forest Trust has had much to learn and, in their evenings and weekends, an inordinate amount to do. Reading through the last chairman's report, nobody could doubt that if we as a society want more Abriachans, we must find a more straightforward, less exhausting, means of achieving them. To illustrate the complexities, let me merely cite the principal funding bodies that have contributed to the project. There are as many again who have given generously from their lesser resources. Remember that every funding body has, properly, its own rules of audit and account. They are: MFST, Forestry Commission through the Woodland Grant Scheme, Rural Challenge, Landfill Tax Redistribution, Objective 1, Highlands and Islands Land Unit, SNH and Leader 2.

I have spoken only about the woodlands. You must also picture a mass of activity concerning the village hall, footpaths, a bird hide, archaeology, chainsaw training and a great deal of good fun. This is a community rediscovering its vigour.

38. CUMBERNAULD GREENSPACES
Scottish Wildlife Trust
Open

Part of the 'New Town' philosophy, going back to Ebenezer Howard, Letchworth, Welwyn Garden City and all that, was the need for generous quantities of trees. They were needed as individuals, along roads, cyclepaths, footpaths and in among the houses, civic buildings, industrial units, shops . . . everywhere. They were also needed as woodlands, small and large, to provide shelter, cover from view and a filter for traffic noise and pollution. These ideas underpin the trees of Cumbernauld. The inspirational text may have been Brenda Colvin's *Trees for Town and Country* (1947). The mood of the time is caught admirably in Nan Fairbrother's influential *New Lives, New Landscapes* (1970).

Whatever you may think about the social, political or economic performance of Cumbernauld, the tree planting has been spectacularly successful in the simple sense that what the Cumbernauld Development Corporation (CDC) set out to do has been achieved. (The future of too many of the individual trees has, alas, been compromised by the grass cutters thrashing their boles, but that is another story.) Much of the success is down to the CDC appointing Peter Youngman as landscape architect and Ian Pollock, an ex-Forestry Commission man, as principal forester. He brought with him proven, uncomplicated forestry techniques and stayed with the project for 25 years. It is, or should be, a simple adage in Scotland – get the mass shelter established before you start thinking about the fancy stuff.

As the CDC was being wound up, it was agreed with the Scottish Office that a number of assets could be disposed of to appropriate bodies. Under this dispensation, some 300 ha of woodland came to the Scottish Wildlife Trust together with a capital endowment of £800,000, the income from which helps to fund the management of the woods. The MFST, during its brief existence, has also contributed generously.

A glance at the list of 95 reserves owned by the Scottish Wildlife Trust in 1994 shows that they are predominantly places like the Montrose Basin or the Loch of the Lowes or Gight Woods where there was an existing, manifest wildlife or conservation value. Much of the Cumbernauld woodland does not have that background. Its acquisition was thus a significant additional thrust of policy for the Trust. What they have acquired here is largely *potential* wildlife value. They have set themselves the admirable long-term task of realising that potential. The 65,000 inhabitants of Cumbernauld have already benefited from the existence of the woodland and the incidental wildlife that came along with it. If all goes to plan, which is by no means certain around any urban fringe, they are set to benefit further from this deliberate widening of the objectives.

These are woodlands for the community.

39. DUNNIKIER WOODS, KIRKCALDY
Fife Council
Open

After the last war Kirkcaldy Town Council bought Dunnikier House and Estate – built for the Oswald family in the 1830s – which were then beyond the northern boundary of the town. Over the decades this land has been developed and there is now housing, a high school complete with playing fields, a golf course, a caravan park, a crematorium and so forth. Dunnikier House has become a hotel. All these developments seem to be in good order. The land left over – essentially the old estate woodland – is, however, far from in good order.

Under the banner of Fife Millennium Forest, with approximately matching funding from the MFST, the local authority has launched a project to try to repair over half a century of neglect of management in these woods and two steep-sided dens leading down from Dunnikier to the town. It is a tall order and it will take a steady nerve to see the project through. Woodland management is seldom easy or cheap in the most

ABOVE: 1. Ballochbuie Native Pinewood

BELOW: 8. Rassal Ashwood, National Nature Reserve, Wester Ross

ABOVE: 9. Morrone Birkwood, National Nature Reserve, Braemar

12. Sessile oak, Meads of St John, Darnaway Estate, Nairn

14. Ash, Bush Estate

BELOW: 16. Aspen,
Boat of Garten

ABOVE: 23. Creag Meagaidh, National Nature Reserve, Glen Spean

BELOW: 33. Scots pine, Culbin Forest, Moray and Nairn

ABOVE: 37. Abriachan Forest Trust, Inverness-shire

LEFT: 42. King Boris's fir, Stonefield Castle Hotel, Tarbert, Argyll

ABOVE: 44. Caucasian fir, Dunkeld Cathedral

BELOW: 47. Cedar of Lebanon, Dalkeith Country Park, Midlothian

50. Maidenhair tree, Dalkeith
Country Park, Midlothian

BELOW: 54. Dawn redwood,
Royal Botanic Garden
Edinburgh

59. Jeffrey's pine, Scone Palace, Perth

BELOW: 60. Montezuma pine,
Cairnsmore, Newton Stewart

favourable circumstances. Woodland management on the urban fringe requires unusually long-term commitment and resources. The rewards are commensurate. Three hectares of heavily used, even abused, woodland is worth any amount of the distant countryside. A shopping trolley in the burn or a tatty old swing rope on a tree are, of course, eyesores, but they are much more importantly symbols of community need and opportunity.

A major asset to the project is the project officer, John Bell. He was born and lived alongside these woods, he walked to the high school, he played all the days of his youth among the project areas, he knows as well as anyone the value of perpetuating what was there for him to enjoy.

I hope fervently that he and the project succeed. If it does, it will be long after the millennium has receded into the mists of memory.

40. EDINBURGH COMMUNITY WOODS
Edinburgh Urban Forestry Project, City of Edinburgh Council
Open

To fly into Edinburgh on a clear day is to see, aside from the familiar defining landmarks, that swathes of the city are more or less treeless. This £1.5 million project has set out to plant new woodlands (woodlets might be a better term) and stand-alone trees right across the city, but particularly where there is least greenery. Most of the 85 sites are in public ownership and include parks, school grounds and golf courses. The highest concentration is at Craigmillar, where the need is greatest. This was the successful springboard into the later and larger project. At the finish, woodland cover in Edinburgh will have increased by 100 ha.

Most of the new trees are natives – birch, rowan, Scots pine, oak, gean, holly and so forth. Most are planted a couple of metres apart. All have been discussed with the local community and a good many have been planted by local children and others. Not everyone is happy. There are folk who dislike long grass and thistles. Wayward golfers cannot find their balls. A few people regard all woodland as the inevitable haunt of undesirables. Overall, however, new greenery is welcome.

The project fits snugly into the principal objective of the MFST: to help develop a permanent, pleasurable green asset for the community. The idea has a few, but far too few, precedents in Scotland. I think for example of Quarry Wood on the western edge of Elgin, which has long been a pleasant place for the citizens to enjoy.

The funding for the Edinburgh project has come from these eight sources:

> Millennium Forest for Scotland Trust – £540,000
> City of Edinburgh Council – £533,000
> Lothian and Edinburgh Enterprise Ltd – £160,000
> Forestry Commission – £147,000
> Scottish Natural Heritage – £35,000
> Wester Hailes Land Use Unit – £26,000
> Craigmillar Initiative – £12,000
> Other – £26,000
> Total – £1,479,000

Inevitably and properly, hundreds of people have become involved. It is right, however, to name as driving forces for the Edinburgh Urban Forestry Project, David Jamieson, Frances Jarvie and Karen Hay, who showed me round with much good humour and *élan*.

PARTICULAR CONIFERS

41. EUROPEAN SILVER FIR *ABIES ALBA*
ARDKINGLAS WOODLAND GARDEN, CAIRNDOW,
ARGYLL
Mr John Noble
Open

For British foresters, the European silver fir was a species of great promise that failed in our conditions. It is thus tantalising to see it, vigorous, healthy and a mainstay of a vibrant sawmilling industry in its homelands, including the Jura, the Alps, the Tatra and the mountains of the Balkans. In classical Greece it was the preferred species for building triremes. It was introduced to Britain in 1603. The trees above the deer fence at Dawyck Botanic Garden near Peebles are the first in Scotland, planted in 1680. Most were lost in the 1968 gale. It must have been tempting to fell the few battered remainders. I am grateful to whoever decided to leave them. There is much to be said for endurance.

For the first century or so, the European silver fir grew faster here than any other tree and, for a while, became the tallest. Even in 1885 Hutchison could still describe it as not supplanted by 'new-fangled introductions' but soon the full potential of many of the conifers from north-west America began to be realised. Finally, sadly, *Abies alba* was found to be seriously susceptible to a woolly aphid. It is now exceptional to see young silver firs except as scattered regeneration from old survivors. One happy exception is the beech and silver fir

wood on the bank above the road into the Dunkeld House Hotel.

It is tempting to assume that trees from Europe will grow better here than trees from further away. What matters is not, however, proximity, but climatic fit. It is not surprising, therefore, that a species from the continental climate of middle Europe should do less well than one from the mild, wet, oceanic climate of the Pacific coast of America.

There are many imposing trees (and rhododendrons) in the woodland garden at Ardkinglas at the head of Loch Fyne, none more remarkable than this European silver fir. It is four-stemmed and so cannot be compared with single-boled trees, but it is legitimate to examine the relative growth. It had a girth in 1905 of 21 ft; it is now 31 ft. This is an astonishing rate of growth for an old tree. There is a powerful photograph of the tree in Thomas Pakenham's coffee table book *Meetings with Remarkable Trees*.

42. KING BORIS'S FIR *ABIES BORISII-REGIS*
STONEFIELD CASTLE HOTEL, TARBERT, ARGYLL
Stonefield Castle Hotel Group
Gardens open all year dawn to dusk
(See first photo section)

When it comes to conifers, the difficulties facing the amateur taxonomist are numerous. At least with broadleaves you can press and store the leaves more or less indefinitely, thus building a reference collection. In the process you discover that a surprising number of trees in prestigious collections are wrongly labelled. It takes somewhere of the maturity of the RBGE to acknowledge that they don't know. One of my favourite labels at Inverleith states only the genus, *Betula*, with no attempt to hazard a guess at the species. With conifers, the needles fall off within a week or two and their arrangement, which is often diagnostic, is lost. That is, if you can reach the shoots in the first place. Then the tree can look distinctly untypical if it is growing in less than ideal conditions. These problems are exacerbated with silver firs because the cones, if present, are almost invariably in the upper crown and fall to bits while still on the tree. Pines, spruces and the like helpfully drop their identifiable and storable cones intact.

The most secure route to identification of conifers, although time-consuming and time-limited, is to hasten, with a fresh shoot in hand, to the nearest reliably labelled collection and make comparison. I was assured by a top botanist not long ago that this is what top botanists do. You can also make a photocopy of the shoot as a simple, helpful aide-memoire. This may raise a few eyebrows at your local copy shop but it is five pence very well spent.

With all this in mind, it is a red-letter day to encounter a fully grown, utterly characteristic specimen of an uncommon conifer. It is maximum bonus points if the tree is, as is the King Boris's fir at Stonefield, visible from tip to toe, round and straight as a ship's mast, completely matching the description in Forestry Commission Booklet 33, *Conifers in the British Isles*, and the biggest in Britain. It is on the right coming in the main drive to Stonefield, the first of many excellent trees around the policies. It is unhelpful, though forgivable, that the label says *Abies nordmanniana*.

The books will tell you that King Boris's fir grows in Pindus, Olympia, Athos and the Isle of Thasor. The inestimable W.T. Stearn will then tell you that the Boris in question was Tsar Boris III of Bulgaria (1894–1943) who came to the throne after the abdication of his father Tsar Ferdinand I in 1918.

43. GRAND FIR *ABIES GRANDIS*
DIANA'S GROVE, BLAIR CASTLE, BLAIR ATHOL
Mrs Sarah Troughton
Opening hours as for the Castle

Twenty years ago, when I knew about such things, there was a rule of thumb that there had to be a minimum annual sawlog production of 20,000 cubic metres of a particular species within a reasonable distance of a sawmill before the miller would attempt to market that species separately. No doubt, given the thirst of commerce for simplicity and scale, the minimum is now a good deal more. Whatever it is, very few species qualify. Even Scots pine, a fine and traditional timber has a struggle. The sawmilling industry in Scotland is based almost exclusively on Sitka spruce because this was virtually the only tree that would grow successfully on the poor sites made available to forestry over the last 70 years or so. Let forestry come down the hill a bit, make some inroads into marginal agriculture and we could have a zone of highly productive Douglas fir below the spruce mingled, of course, with birch and the like.

One of the 'minor species' which came under scrutiny to see if it should not be planted on a wider scale was grand fir, hardly surprising since on a good site grand fir grows like a tree possessed. Alas for such speculations, grand fir is an unexciting wood. Donald Culross Peattie says, 'too soft, yet too heavy in proportion to its little strength . . . pulpwood offers its only commercial future and there are so many finer pulping species that grand fir is usually left in the forest to make music and distil incense'. He is speaking about the tree in his native North America.

So we are best advised to go on growing grand fir for the beauty of the tree in youth, middle and old age, for the orange scent of the foliage and for its willingness to leap out of the ground on anything like a reasonable site.

There is hardly a collection of conifers anywhere in Scotland without a burgeoning grand fir among them. My favourites are at Abercairney in Perthshire, along the drive at Ardverikie as seen across Loch Laggan, the huge tree at Strone, Cairndow, which was the first in Britain to reach 200 ft but has had the top knocked back, and the 17 grand firs in Diana's Grove behind the castle at Blair.

Alan Mitchell was fond of saying that there was more wood per acre in Diana's Grove than anywhere east of the Rockies. He might have added or 'west of Sakhalin Island'. There are about 180 trees in the grove, most of them gigantic, none older than 1872. The tallest grand fir, when measured in 1994 by R. Panting, was 190 ft by 17 ft girth. It is a simple demonstration that Scotland is one of the best places in the world for growing the spruces and firs that have evolved to relish an oceanic climate. Not having a spruce or fir of our own, we had to wait for someone to bring them. There is no better place to break your journey up, or down, the A9.

44. CAUCASIAN FIR *ABIES NORDMANNIANA*
DUNKELD CATHEDRAL
Historic Scotland
Open through the day
(See first photo section)

There are something in the order of 50 species of silver fir in the world. They all grow naturally on mountain ranges in the northern temperate region and are distinguished by the small round scars left after you remove a needle and the upright cones, often purple, which break up on the tree leaving candle-like stalks. A reasonably diligent hunt through the arboreta of Scotland will turn up 30, or a few more. There are 23 at Dawyck alone, some more than 100 ft in the air, some having a struggle to make 40 ft. Most silver firs are very enjoyable in youth or early middle age – vigorous shoots bearing buoyant needles, glossy green on top, often flashing white underneath from lines of silver stomata. A number of silver firs also smell delicious. Lovely fir smells of oranges, Maries fir of ginger and Sakhalin fir of something exotic, even illegal.

By middle age, all too often the symmetry and glowing good health of the young silver fir begins to dissipate. At worst the crown becomes anaemic and branchy. Even when the needles on current shoots remain vigorous, the lower branches will often die or the central axis be lost to a group of leaders. Overconing, especially in noble fir, can look distinctly ugly. The tallest, like grand fir and European silver fir, growing into the wind above the main canopy, will often lose their centrality and their shape.

There are exceptions. The red firs at Dunkeld House and Blair Castle are still superb, almost from tip to toe. The storm-battered hulks of the 1680 European silver firs above the fence at Dawyck have assumed the pathos and endurance of broken royalty.

The shining exception to most of these generalities is the Caucasian fir, named, in Latin, after the Finnish Professor Nordmann, who proposed it as a separate species in 1837. Shortly after, in 1848, it was introduced to Britain by the entrepreneurial Lawsons of Edinburgh. The 1855 tree at Dawyck has gone, as has the 1860 tree at Scone but you will still see big vigorous trees at Arisaig Hotel, Mallaig, just into the drive at Meikleour, at Dunans, Glendaruel, at Wester Elchies on the banks of the Spey and, best of all, this luxuriant tree in the mown grass on the lower terrace at Dunkeld Cathedral. The needles at the end of each shoot point softly forward, like a cat's paw.

45. MONKEY PUZZLE *ARAUCARIA ARAUCANA*
ARDMHOR, BARRA
Scottish Executive, Rural Affairs Department
Open

In any competition to name the most exotic-looking tree introduced into the British Isles, the outright winner must surely be the monkey puzzle. A curious sociological quirk is that, although enthusiasm for this oddity has waxed and waned over the two centuries since it was first grown, it has always been more popular here than anywhere else on earth, other than its native Chile.

I have never seen monkey puzzles in their natural habitat, having to be content with photographs and discussions with friends who have made the slightly hairy expedition. All witnesses agree that the trees, which grow from about 1,200 m up to the snowline, often in soils that look like clinker, tend to keep their reptilian distance from each other and never lose that sense of strangeness and gawky symmetry. Not numerous in the wild, it may be the case that there are now as many in these islands as in Chile.

The monkey puzzle has proved popular in Scotland. After a slow start, it grows well almost everywhere. I remember a tree almost at high water mark beyond Nairn – extraordinary that a tree from the high Andes should cope with salt spray. There are excellent trees at Whittingehame and Craigievar in the east and at Cairnsmore, Castle Kennedy and Armadale in the west. But the tree that has delighted me most is this totally unexpected, unmistakable silhouette beside the road in a sheltered corner of north-east Barra. I saw it first in the company of Niall Macpherson, who was at that point driving the post bus and declaring that 'foresters travel free'. A sentiment too infrequently expressed, but then the man has himself embarked on some ambitious planting at Aros Cottage. The tree was already large when he knew it as a boy. There were three until quite recently.

You need a male and a female growing together to make the huge football of a cone. After two or three years the cones break up, shedding anything up to 200 large seeds. (They are edible raw but a lot better if pan roasted in a little olive oil.) I have found regeneration at a number of places on the west coast, though nothing like the acre or so of uneven-aged, young monkey puzzle I knew in Devon. Seed that I collected from underneath a tree at Brodie Castle, Nairn, grew with ease. Two of the resultant youngsters were, in 1993 at least, growing contentedly in the garden of a friend outside Reykjavik.

46. DEODAR *CEDRUS DEODARA*
SCOTTISH NATURAL HERITAGE HEADQUARTERS,
HOPE TERRACE, THE GRANGE, EDINBURGH
Scottish Natural Heritage
Private but readily visible from Blackford Road

The deodar, which is the north Indian name for this valuable tree, grows along the entire western Himalayas at altitudes between 1,200 and 3,000 metres. (Put two or three Munros on top of each other.) The tree associates of the deodar at lower elevations can only survive in the very mildest parts of Britain. Associates in the 1,800 to 2,400 metre band –

Bhutan pine, pindrow fir, Himalayan cypress – grow well in Scotland, though only Bhutan pine is commonly encountered and not so commonly as the deodar.

This is one of only four true cedars in the world. The cones are diagnostic: fat barrels sitting upright like Russian dolls on the sweeping branches. They are common on the other three cedars, from Lebanon, Cyprus and Morocco, respectively, but uncommon or very uncommon on the deodar. In fact if you encounter a biggish, coneless cedar, it is likely to be this one. It has also longer needles, drooping end shoots and a drooping leader or leaders. After a slow start the deodar grows at a rattling good pace but height growth more or less ceases somewhere in the bracket 80–100 ft.

Introduction of the deodar is attributed to the Honourable Leslie Melville, who sent seeds home in 1831. Many trees were raised from this seed and widely distributed. It quickly became apparent that these handsome trees were hardy, and by the 1850s they were being grown almost everywhere. There is no preference for east or west, north or south. You will see fine deodars at, for example, Capenoch in Dumfries-shire, Blairquhan in Ayrshire, Inverary, Conon Bridge, Rossie Priory in Perthshire and Smeaton Hepburn, East Lothian.

The dates of introductions of some of the trees from India and Burma were these:

> 1807 *Pinus roxburghii* – None in Scotland?
> 1818 *Picea smithiana* – Original tree still at Hopetoun
> 1820 *Sorbus cuspidata* – Uncommon despite its quality
> 1822 *Abies spectabilis* – Good trees at Fasque, Keir House, Inverary
> 1823 *Pinus wallichiana* – Introduced by A.B. Lambert. Fairly common
> 1824 *Cotoneaster frigidus* – Locally common
> 1831 *Cedrus deodara* – See text
> 1837 *Abies pindrow* – Good trees at Smeaton and Whittingehame

1848 *Larix griffithii* – Flowerdale. Recent planting at Benmore

1849 *Betula utilis* – Introduced by Sir Joseph Hooker

1851 *Aesculus indica* – Occasional and in some surprising places

1860 *Prunus cornuta* – Rare, which is odd given a fine tree in the RBGE

1865 *Magnolia campbellii* – When happy, the best of all the magnolias

The quartet in the back garden of SNH headquarters in Edinburgh are as characteristic as you could wish of a Victorian planting.

47. CEDAR OF LEBANON *CEDRUS LIBANI* DALKEITH COUNTRY PARK, MIDLOTHIAN
Buccleuch Estates
Grounds open dawn to dusk
(See first photo section)

I am very fond of the Dalkeith Estate, having worked there while a student, under the tutelage of an indomitable ganger by the name of Geordie and a famous head forester called Willie Mowat. No recommendation is really necessary given that the house is 'one of Scotland's premier classical houses refashioned from one of its greatest Renaissance houses' (presently occupied by the University of Wisconsin), the Montague Bridge was designed by Robert Adam and built by his brother James and it is home to the wonders of the Dalkeith Old Wood, celebrated elsewhere in these pages.

Among the fine trees at Dalkeith are two Lebanon cedars at the back of, and appearing over, the stables designed by William Adam in 1740. Both are over 80 ft. The larger has a girth now approaching 20 ft and a planting date of 1770. It has a trunk of about 20 ft, being intermediate in form between the 'gun barrels' and the more familiar 'gargantuan bushes' – the two forms of this cedar.

The Lebanon cedar was introduced in the seventeenth century but almost all the early trees were killed by the savage frosts of 1740. One of the exceptions was the Union Cedar planted at Biel, East Lothian, in 1707 by Lord Belhaven in what he considered the first year of Scotland's betrayal. It blew down in 1927 in the full, astonished view of its then owner. He was shaving at the time.

Lebanon cedars are very sensitive to atmospheric pollution so there are no old trees in the city centres. Edinburgh is, however, ringed with huge cedars at Prestonhall House, Arniston, Dalhousie, Hopetoun, Riccarton and others. There remains a splendid tree at Biel, with a girth of 26 ft, often mistaken for the Union cedar.

With good reason, the Atlas cedar from Morocco and the Lebanon are occasionally confused. One helpful guide: the Atlas cedar was not introduced until 1840 and none yet has a girth exceeding 19 ft, which is also the size of the biggest deodar (just west of Inverness). It follows that any cedar over 20 ft must be a Lebanon.

48. WISSEL'S LAWSON CYPRESS *CHAMAECYPARIS LAWSONIANA* 'WISSELII'
LECKMELM, ULLAPOOL
Mr and Mrs Peter Troughton
Opening hours

In the books about trees there is always a section on the false cypresses, *Chamaecyparis*, which many people avoid. The species are similar but, much more confusing, all have given rise to innumerable accidental variants, which, vegetatively propagated by a nursery trade eager to sell novelty, became named cultivars. Each cultivar is genetically identical. There are variations of size from dwarf shrubs to forest trees, variations of colour – green, blue, silvery, gold – and variations of foliage. Altogether they run into several hundred cultivars, perhaps thousands. Leckmelm, on the shores of Loch Broom on the road to Ullapool, is an excellent place to see a collection of false cypresses that have become very substantial trees.

It is tempting to wilt in the face of such near similar variety. A way out of the difficulty is the fruit. No matter the difference in foliage, the fruit remains constant and is generally present on all but very young trees. Another huge help is taste, if you can bring yourself to nibble (and spit out) a spray. A friend who has been eating Lawson cypress all his life is still playing tennis in his 70s, so it may even be health-giving!

Many of the trees at Leckmelm have been made to form multiple trunks by weighing down the shoots in their youth, a favourite Victorian practice. The Hiba, for example, is more a thicket than a tree. This Wissel's cypress, beside the Hiba, is massive, the tallest and the fattest in Britain. The foliage is well out of reach and almost out of detailed scrutiny. When you see it at closer quarters, it is so oddly arranged, so different from the type, that you would be entitled to think it something entirely different.

Just up the road from Leckmelm live Vicky and Tony Schilling. She was one of the founders and he the first chairman of the Tree Register of the British Isles (TROBI). At first TROBI was the repository of Alan Mitchell's tree records. Subsequently, many tree measurers have been contributing results. TROBI has now, fruitfully, entered the world of the Internet. For a modest subscription you can have instant access to the location and dimension of the Champion Trees (for each species the tallest tree and that with the largest girth in Britain is recorded) and, on request, to the records of interest to you for well over 100,000 trees in Britain. Details of membership can be found at www.tree-register.org

49. LEYLAND CYPRESS *X CUPRESSOCYPARIS LEYLANDII*, ACHAMORE GARDEN, ISLE OF GIGHA
Holt Leisure
Open

I have only visited Gigha once, but from that one memorable visit I still have an acute and pleasurable memory of a Leyland cypress hedge. It had been planted a couple of decades earlier by the then owner, Lt.Col Sir James Horlick, around an area known as the 'Hospital'. Plants under stress elsewhere in the gardens were taken to the Hospital to be nursed back to health. When I saw it, the hedge was held to about 15 ft and – this is the heart of my remembered pleasure – to about 18 in. wide. Malcolm McNeill, who, boy and man, has been clipping the hedge for the past 42 years, tells me that it is not what it was – too many salt winds, too much shade and fewer man-hours available. Its decline should by no means discourage you from going to Gigha as there is an abundance of other things to enjoy.

Left to its own devices, as everybody knows, Leyland cypress grows like a Jack's beanstalk. Given a reasonable depth of soil and not too much shade, it will outgrow every other conifer and even keep pace with poplars and eucalypts, except on sites particularly favourable to these greedy feeders. It is prone to blow over inside a century or to have the crown broken by wind or snow. The vigour comes from its being a hybrid. One parent grows in Monterey County, California. The other has a wider distribution, growing best in Vancouver Island and as far south as Oregon but that is still 500 km from Monterey. Thus, the hybrid could only arise once the parents had been brought together by the intervention of a gardener and once they had begun to flower. The first crossing probably occurred, unrecognised, at Rostrevor in Ireland; the best-known and best-documented in 1888 at Leighton Hall, near Welshpool on the Welsh border. The cross will and does differ depending on which species is the female parent.

The message is simple. You can have whatever Leyland cypress you need and like – a 100 ft tree or an 18 in. wide hedge. If it is in the wrong place or mismanaged, then that says something about you, or your neighbour, not about this outstanding newcomer.

Incidentally, Sir James Horlick was the holder of both the Military Cross and the Victoria Medal of Honour from the Royal Horticultural Society. Was he unique?

50. MAIDENHAIR TREE* *GINKGO BILOBA*
DALKEITH COUNTRY PARK, MIDLOTHIAN
Buccleuch Estates Ltd
Grounds open dawn to dusk
(See first photo section)

I grew a maidenhair or *Ginkgo* in our Elgin garden. After half a dozen years, although hardy, healthy and a daily pleasure for its ancient-looking twigs and leathery fan-shaped, fan-veined leaves, like those of the maidenhair fern, it was still short of waist high. There are a fair number of *Ginkgo*s in Edinburgh in the height bracket 15–25 ft, slow growing and with a tendency, shared with trees further south, for the terminal buds not to produce extension shoots. This can lead to a confused tangle. Nonetheless, almost every *Ginkgo* is distinctive and distinguished, the only tree of its kind in the world, neither conifer nor broadleaf – fossil history in front of your eyes. The tree at Dalkeith, overhanging the wall between the Stables and the Laundry Bridge is, at 6 ft girth, perhaps as large as they will grow in Scotland. I don't know the age.

Ginkgo is, apparently, a distortion of the Japanese 'gin' (silver), 'kyo' (apricot). The fruit is a small yellow-green 'plum' with a pulpy inner, before you get to the silver nut. It is described variously, as 'evil-

---

* This species, which is included here with the conifers, is classed botanically in the same phylum as conifers and cycads, but pre-dates conifers. It is the sole survivor of a large group of plants from 180 million years ago (the Jurassic and Cretaceous periods).

smelling', 'malodorous', 'putrid' or 'rancid'. It is edible, though, and much used in Chinese medicine and tonic foods. You need a male and a female tree to make the fruit, or you must graft a male branch on to a female tree, a solution often practised in Japan, apparently. I do not know how far south you have to go to find the fruit in Britain. I think it may be Watford. Fruit is common enough in the warmest parts of Europe, in Toulouse for example.

After dominating the world during the Jurassic period, *Ginkgo* became confined to small areas of China. In historic times it has been planted extensively over China and Japan and more recently in Europe and North America. Male trees make surprising and splendid street trees, in Paris, for example, or Boston, Massachusetts, or Cambridge, England.

There are few wholefood stores, even supermarkets, which do not carry preparations of *Ginkgo*. The claims are impressive and not unlike those for snake oil. You can try it yourself by collecting and drying the leaves. Put one ounce in one pint of water. Simmer for five minutes and then cool. Drink a quarter-cup, warm, morning and evening and live longer.

51. MOUNTAIN HEMLOCK *HESPEROPEUCE MERTENSIANA*
FAIRBURN HOUSE, MUIR OF ORD, EASTER ROSS
Mr Clifford Davison
Private but visitors welcome if they ask

There is a crescent of remarkable tree places just west of the heads of the Beauly and Cromarty Firths. All have their surprises and delights but, for sheer numbers of huge conifers packed into a few hectares, Fairburn is in the class of Diana's Grove, Blair Atholl, Strone or, not too far away, Reelig or Moniac Glen. (This last is unimaginatively signposted as Forest Walks when it should be trumpeted as the Scottish Everglades.)

Fairburn House is now a home for the physically and mentally disabled. When you go in to ask permission to see the trees you will come out, as I did, humble and hugely admiring of everyone who dedicates their time, humanity and energy to such caring work.

Amongst all the splendours of Fairburn are several mountain hemlocks. One of them is said to be the tallest in Britain, but the company it keeps is so monumental that even at 120 ft it does not look that impressive. I actually prefer the younger trees, furnished to ground level where you can enjoy the elegant arrangement of the needles, something between a cedar and a larch.

Taxonomists have recently taken the mountain hemlock out of the genus *Tsuga* and put it under *Hesperopeuce*. For once, the rest of us can see the logic of the decision as it has always looked the odd one out among the other hemlocks.

The progress of the trees at Fairburn has been admired and plotted by the Stirling family, who planted them there, and by a succession of tree experts. The latest in this line of knowledgeable enthusiasts is John Miller from Alness. He has brought his experience together into an entertaining booklet entitled *Trees of the Northern Highlands*. Everyone with an interest in trees north and west of, and within, Inverness should possess a copy.

As the name suggests, this is very much a mountain tree. It grows all the way down the Cascades and the Sierra Nevada from Alaska to California. Donald Culross Peattie particularly admired the mountain hemlock at the limits of its altitude: 'The trunk creeping along the rocks or struggling erect, may be no higher than a man . . . the boles apt to be immensely thick in proportion to their height.'

52. LARCHES *LARIX SPP.*
DUNKELD HOUSE HOTEL, DUNKELD,
Owned by Hilton Hotels

Kennel Bank, above the drive into the hotel, owned by Forest
Enterprise

Open

I had supposed that everyone thought the introduction of European
larch into Scotland an unmixed blessing. I was wrong. Here is Lord
Cockburn at Aviemore in April 1839: 'We must begin by clearing the
country of at least nineteen parts out of every twenty of that abominable
larch with which it pleased the late Rothiemurchus, as it still pleases
many Highland lairds, to stiffen and blacken the land.' I owe this nugget
of Scottish woodland history to Professor Chris Smout of St Andrews
University, who, over the last decade or so, has brought his formidable
erudition and energy to bear on the subject and has inspired and
encouraged others to follow suit.

I do think Lord Cockburn was the exception. Most of us enjoy larch
whether as an isolated, wind-pruned veteran of the storms, or turned
fresh apple-green on a Perthshire hillside one warm spring day, or
changing a brown winter woodland track to orange-russet with fallen
needles. Foresters speak of larch as 'an honorary broadleaf'.

Larch timber was, for its strength and durability, preferred for estate
purposes and for the craft of wooden boat building. For the time being,
the market is little interested in timbers of quality, unless they come in
bulk and uniformity. Am I an incurable optimist in supposing that
further developments in electronic scanning, mechanical stress grading,
computer control and the like might bring a return to marketing
particular woods?

Dunkeld is the epicentre of the Scottish larch story. Behind the
cathedral is one of the trees brought from London during 1737 'in a
hamper' by John Menzies of Culdars (now Meggernie) for James, 2nd
Duke of Atholl, a number of other friends and himself. This is the last

of five planted on the site and, since the site is favourable for tree growth, it is a whopper and highly photogenic. The surrounds are unappealing but, happily, Hilton Hotels have plans to bring them up to their own high standards.

The 2nd Duke, his son John and particularly his grandson, also John, the 4th Duke, became interested and eventually absorbed in planting European larch on the hills of Atholl. By 1830 their combined planting numbered 14 million. Among them were the supreme 1750 trees on Kennel Bank beside the drive into the hotel. By 1904 pollen from these had fertilised flowers on the eleven 1887 Japanese larch below and produced the first Dunkeld hybrid larches, more vigorous and with the better qualities of both parents. These too you can see, across the field from the drive along the path known as Bishop's Walk.

53. SIKKIM LARCH *LARIX GRIFFITHIANA*
YOUNGER BOTANIC GARDEN, BENMORE, BY
DUNOON
Part of the Royal Botanic Garden Edinburgh
Opening hours

Benmore has everything you could wish: a distinguished past, a secure present and an adventurous future. It is a place that you could visit every day of the year and still miss something. If you can take your eyes off the stunning trees for a moment you are looking at, in combination with the parent garden in Edinburgh, the richest assembly of species rhododendrons in the world.

The part of this huge enterprise that I particularly want to celebrate is one of the most recent initiatives – the Bhutan Glade. To reach the bottom of the glade you go up the sheltered Glen Massan under huge, well-spaced, north-west American conifers. Try to go in June when the new growth of ferns, soft grass and forest herbs is vibrant and untrodden.

The adventure is to recreate, in the mild, moist, well-matched climate of Benmore, something of the experience of moving up through the tree and shrub altitudinal zones of Bhutan. You start on the glen floor with *Populus ciliata* and a very odd but handsome tree called *Tetracentron sinense* – not to be seen elsewhere in Scotland, I think, except in the RBGE. You climb up over some entertaining paths, wooden steps and bridges through zones dominated respectively by an elegant five-needled pine, this Sikkim larch and one of the burgeoning long-needled silver firs that are a specialty of the Himalayas. You finish in what will, in due course, be juniper scrub. What makes this project so satisfactory and so much a precedent to follow is that the trees and shrubs come from seed collected in the wild by botanists from the staff of the RBGE, who have themselves been compiling the flora of Bhutan. This is botanical research, conservation and pleasure for the rest of us run handsomely together.

This larch, very seldom seen in Scotland, has long, wandering, horizontal branches, widely spaced, pendulous twigs and unmistakable big cones. Jim Paterson tells me that there is a fine tree at Flowerdale House in Wester Ross. It was named, in Latin, for Dr William Griffiths (1810–1879) who 'discovered' the tree during his explorations of Sikkim and Bhutan.

54. DAWN REDWOOD *METASEQUOIA GLYPTOSTROBOIDES*
ROYAL BOTANIC GARDEN EDINBURGH
Royal Botanic Garden (also in many largish gardens)
Opening hours
(See first photo section)

It is not merely difficult, it is impossible to exaggerate the extraordinary facts that surround the dawn redwood. For people who knew about such things it was merely a well-understood fossil of the Liassic up to the Pliocene periods, turning up in northern hemisphere deposits in Canada, Greenland, Spitzbergen and eastwards. It had been safely extinct for a couple of million years until a botanist/forester from Peking National Central University came across three trees in 1941. It was tantamount to swimming casually into a colony of Loch Ness monsters.

The locals, who did not know that they were the curators of a phenomenon, told him that the tree was called Shui-hsa, which translates, somewhat unexcitingly, as water fir. In due course it became apparent that there was a valley, not far away, containing over 1,000 substantial trees together with a mass of natural regeneration. The valley lies on the border between Szechuan and Hupeh, an area cultivated for millennia and extensively explored by European plant hunters.

By autumn 1947, not only had the tree acquired the rather splendid name of dawn redwood, but Dr E.D. Merrill, then Director of the Arnold Arboretum in Boston, had acquired quantities of seeds and, with great generosity, distributed them far and wide. You will find the trees growing well all over Scotland but not, it must be admitted, as vigorously as you will find them in the Cambridge colleges, say, or St James's Park, London, where greater summer warmth is combined with moist conditions underfoot.

There are two quirky things to know about the dawn redwood. First, unlike almost every tree you can think of, the buds are underneath the axils of the shoots rather than on top. Second, unlike almost all conifers, it is very easy to strike from cuttings. I know three Scottish trees which started life as cuttings standing in water in milk bottles on a kitchen window sill.

There are several in the RBGE, which is a handy place to make comparison with the not dissimilar, equally feathery, swamp cypress. Scone is another place to look. The dawn redwoods are between the Jeffrey's pine and the quartet of gigantic Sitka.

55. SERBIAN SPRUCE *PICEA OMORIKA*
MURTHLY CASTLE, BY DUNKELD
Mr Robert Steuart Fothringham
Private but access by written permission

I have been mildly critical in my time of Scott Leathart's *Whence Our Trees* (1991) because of the misspellings of Scottish trees. It will not do, for example, to have Smeddon, Pitcarmich, Elchres and Kippencross for Smeaton, Pitcarmick, Elchies and Kippenross. But these are minor blemishes in an otherwise admirable book. He is particularly strong on the natural ecology of the trees he discusses, the geology, soils, elevations and tree floras.

I have known since David Paterson studied the species on site, while he was an Edinburgh post-graduate in the 1950s, that this spruce is confined, as a natural tree, to a tiny area of Bosnia-Herzegovina and

Serbia. It could not move north as the ice melted because other tree species were more efficient at exploiting the plains. I did not appreciate, however, until reading Scott Leathart, that it was a relict species, meaning one which had survived the Ice Age more or less in the same place.

It comes as a surprise to foresters, supposing that spruces are trees of wet or wettish places, to realise that Serbian spruces grow on limestone mountains, high up by themselves or lower down in mixture with species like pines, silver fir and beech. Even more interesting is the fact that these are flat-needled spruces, thousands and thousands of miles away from their nearest cousins.

Serbian spruce might have made it into the big time of spruces in Britain had it not been for the rude vigour of Sitka and the, to my mind often misguided, enthusiasm for Norway spruce. You will find it occasionally planted by the half-hectare but more usually as an individual or in a small group in arboreta, parks and gardens. For these purposes it is seldom less than admirable: a good-growing, healthy, remarkably slender spruce, impervious as to soil and late frosts. The silhouette of a mature tree is like a slim Chinese pagoda.

There are none better than the three near the river at Murthly. To get there you must go through a large grove of huge, widely spaced conifers which is in the blue riband class.

56. SITKA SPRUCE *PICEA SITCHENSIS*
RANDOLPH'S LEAP, RIVER FINDHORN (BETWEEN LOGIE AND RELUGAS)
Alasdair Laing, Logie Estate
Private but in full view from this renowned beauty spot

By any reckoning, Sitka spruce is the most important addition ever to the tree flora of Scotland. It has evolved over millions of years to fit the mild, moist, windy climate to be found over some 2,500 km of the Pacific coast of North America and finds the mild, moist, windy climate of Scotland, particularly western Scotland, a home from home. In a

sense it is more at home than Scots pine or oak, which are continental trees having a bit of a struggle here at the oceanic edge of their distributions.

On all but the most fertile and infertile sites, Sitka will outgrow every other tree. No Scottish Sitka is older than 1832, yet a dozen are already over 200 ft high and several score have a girth over 20 ft.

None of this would be relevant if Sitka was a worthless timber. It is, conversely, the mainstay of the British sawmilling industry, which now, thanks to a huge investment in computer-aided technology, supplies about a quarter of our sawn softwood demand. The long fibre of Sitka spruce is especially useful in the manufacture of board, pulp and paper. Sitka was the favoured species for aircraft construction. In the USA it is still a preferred wood for violins. I owe to Ian Darwin Edwards, Director of the Public Programme at the RBGE, the information that Native Americans used the resin as 'an all-purpose adhesive to caulk holes in boats, cure carbuncles or as chewing gum'. If all else fails, you can, apparently, make the roots into a waterproof hat.

So why do some people have a problem with a tree flourishing in Scotland when it is an icon for conservationists back in its home country? I can suggest three legitimate reasons and explain why each is losing its force.

First, because of the hold of agriculture throughout its expansion phase, the Forestry Commission, and later private planters, were forced on to ground which would have been better left unplanted, whether taking economic or aesthetic views into consideration. As these places are felled, they should be allowed to develop into birchwoods. Second, the Sitka plantations were too often arranged without aesthetic sympathy to the features on the ground and as monocultures from which everything else had been, expensively, excluded. Thanks to enlightened philosophies and practices the next generation is not, and will not be, like that. Third, carried away with misplaced zeal, too many foresters planted Sitka within or too close to invaluable native woodlands. Such practices ceased decades ago, and past mistakes are being corrected, particularly now with assistance from the MFST.

Sitka spruce is everywhere in Scotland and to most Scots and visitors it is simply part of the scenery. Spectacularly large Sitka are not hard to find. If you like your trees not only tall but shapely and in a perfect setting, try this specimen overlooking a gorge of the Findhorn at Randolph's Leap, where the water creams past like a perfect bowl of Guinness. As a bonus the tree alongside the giant Sitka is a giant Douglas fir. Both are at or just over 200 ft high.

57. MORINDA SPRUCE *PICEA SMITHIANA*
HOPETOUN HOUSE, SOUTH QUEENSFERRY
Hopetoun House Trust
Opening hours

As a rule, spruces are not happy too close to the east coast. They do not like the cold winds and they need more moisture than is available here. This is generally true of the morinda spruce: you have to go somewhere like Taymouth Castle, Kenmore, to see the tree at its best, but I must include the morindas at Hopetoun not only because they are bonny but because they were the first to be grown in Britain.

In 1818 Dr George Govan (1787–1867), later first superintendent of the Botanical Garden at Saharanpur, sent cones home to his father, also Dr Govan, of Cupar, Fife. Dr Govan senior gave the cones to the Earl of Hopetoun, whose gardener James Smith germinated some seeds during that year. The resultant seedlings were kept in pots until 1820 or 1821 – authorities differ – when two were planted out in the kitchen garden at Hopetoun, one sent to the Royal Horticultural Society and three to the RBGE. In order to increase the stock James Smith grafted morinda cuttings on to Norway spruce and in 1829 planted one beside the seedlings and three in the gardens west of the house. All six were still there in 1999. The two trees from seedlings have been measured in 1837, 1891, 1911, 1931, 1971 and 1993, usually in imperial to make comparison easy. The larger is now just short of 90 ft tall and 11 ft girth.

Contrast these with 128 ft and 15 ft for the biggest in Britain and some measure of the disadvantage of the east coast becomes apparent.

The morinda spruce grows naturally in the mountains of Nepal, Kashmir and Afghanistan, consorting with splendid trees like the deodar, Bhutan pine and pindrow fir. In full health and vigour it is the second most elegant spruce, with long needles on long hanging branches. The first is Brewer's spruce from North America.

The tree is named in Latin after Sir James Smith (1759–1828), first president of the Linnean Society. Morinda derives from *morus*, mulberry and *indicus*, Indian. Indian mulberry, however, seems remarkably inappropriate.

58. AROLLA PINE *PINUS CEMBRA*
AIRTHREY CASTLE, STIRLING UNIVERSITY
Stirling University
Open

What I like, what I suppose everybody likes, about the arolla pine (or cembran pine or Swiss stone pine) is that the cones are shed before they open, most unusual behaviour for a pine and not shared with any other that you will meet in Scotland. If you are quick you can find the cones beneath old trees, still with the seeds intact. More usually, small mammals will have got there first and left only the neat pockets where the seeds were housed.

The books all say that the tree was introduced from Europe to his Hounslow estate by the Duke of Argyll in 1746, leaving us to wonder why Argyll was not too busy quelling, as he saw it, the rebellion of that calamitous year. It does not grow particularly old or tall, 100 ft is exceptional, but chugs on much the same north or south, east or west – Dumfriesshire, Ayrshire, Ross, Banff or this tree of ten foot girth at the top of Stirling University campus in the remnants of the Airthrey Castle gardens. Though bearing branches of rich green needles in fives, the overall impression is a dark-green tree, rather stubby in outline.

Pinus cembra (cembra is the Italian name) was one of the first trees to colonise the bare ground behind the retreating central European glaciers. You will find it today in the Alps and Carpathians, consorting with European larch and skiers. A closely related pine covers enormous tracts of Russia and Siberia, where the seeds were, and possibly still are, an important food source for the local population. There is something particularly satisfying about a tree which reduces the risk of avalanches, and feeds mice and men.

It is also the favoured food of that excellent Jay-like bird, the Nutcracker. In the few years each century when Nutcrackers irrupt from their European breeding areas, it is worthwhile for birdwatchers to check their local arolla pines.

59. JEFFREY'S PINE *PINUS JEFFREYI*
SCONE PALACE, PERTH
The Earl of Mansfield
Opening hours
(See first photo section)

If you were parachuted blindfold into the pinetum at Scone Palace you would know exactly where you were in Scotland, probably in the world. There are a number of places with a similar array of conifers but none where they are set out in widely spaced rows over mown grass. The pinetum was started in 1848 by the 3rd Earl of Mansfield when it was becoming clear that the David Douglas introductions were growing spectacularly well, including the Douglas firs from the 1827 seed at Scone itself, which you pass on the way into the arboretum from the car park.

A number of the originals have gone or are no longer looking fully fit but there remains more than a quorum of superb trees, notably the noble firs, four huge Sitka and, for my money, the best of the lot, this 1866 Jeffrey's pine. It is, by some margin, the biggest in Britain, at 120 ft high and 14 ft girth but, as I keep on insisting, it is not size that is crucial but a quality which I think of as 'presence'.

There are Jeffrey's pines which are almost as good at Rossie Priory in Perthshire, beside Castle Menzies near Aberfeldy and at Culcreuch Castle Hotel, beside Fintry in the Campsies. As a young tree Jeffrey's can be confused with ponderosa, another three-needled pine from the western USA. Big trees can usually be separated by the bark, which is nearly black on Jeffrey's but pink or red on ponderosa. Once cones are present the problem ceases. Jeffrey's cones are huge, on the tree or where they have fallen.

The Jeffrey after whom they were named was John Jeffrey, a Scot in the mould of David Douglas and John Muir. He was 24 and working at the RBGE when he was recommended as a seed collector to the Oregon Association, a group of mainly Perthshire landowners, with George Patton of Cairnies and Glenalmond in the lead. He sent home his tenth box of plants and seeds from San Francisco in 1853 and was heard of no more. In all, he introduced 20 new conifers including western hemlock, foxtail pine and this, his own pine. Although not planted out until 1866, it is near certain that the Scone tree came from seed Jeffrey collected in Shasta Valley in October 1852. What better memorial could there be to the man?

Replacement trees have been planted within the pinetum and on land adjoining. The first replacements came from John Horsman, a tree nurseryman who, first at Auchterarder, then at Ardkinglas, grew and sold an astounding array of trees, many from wild collections, all immaculately labelled.

60. MONTEZUMA PINE *PINUS MONTEZUMAE*
CAIRNSMORE, NEWTON STEWART
Mr and Mrs Nigel Champion
Private but adjacent to the drive along which the family allow access
(See first photo section)

Alan Mitchell, working from the Forestry Commission's Research Station at Alice Holt, Farnham, Surrey, devoted almost his entire life to visiting, measuring, cataloguing and publicising the trees of Britain and Ireland. His memory was prodigious. He seemed never to have forgotten a tree or its dimensions. He was in that distinguished line of tree experts from John Claudius Loudon, through Elwes and Henry, to W.J. Bean. He wore sandals without socks whatever the weather. He never went to bed without completing his tree records for the day in his distinctive script. He spoke his mind, indifferent to company, on matters of importance to him – whether on the ecological crime of flooding Upper Teesdale or the aesthetic deficiencies of copper beech or absurd pronouncements by Friends of the Earth about the supposed effects of acid rain on the trees of Britain. He knew what he knew with comprehensive authority. He was never happier than when in among the big conifers of Scotland, particularly if, since he was also a more than competent ornithologist, there were Ospreys about or Crossbills or Crested Tits or a Greenshank on passage.

When Alan Mitchell spoke it was *ex cathedra*. He said of this wonderful pine that it was not only the biggest and best in Scotland but one of the best anywhere in these islands. 'Do not,' he would say, 'pass down the road to Newton Stewart without calling in to make obeisance.' Once seen, a mature Montezuma pine is never to be forgotten. Not only is the beehive shape distinctive but there is no other pine with such long, dense, blue-green needles. Because they are never still, the crown looks like running water. In the right place, which is only in the mildest areas, Montezuma pines put on girth at almost twice the rate of other pines.

61. Austrian pine, Dawyck Botanic
Garden, Stobo, Peebles-shire

BELOW: 67. Swamp cypress,
Bargany Estate, by Girvan

ABOVE: 74. The Corstorphine Sycamore, Corstorphine, Edinburgh (blown down in December 1998)

75. Madrona, Castle Menzies, Weem, by Aberfeldy

76. Spanish chestnut, 'Rizzio's Oak', Melville Castle, Dalkeith

BELOW: 77. Katsura, Battleby, Redgorton, Perthshire

82. Cider gum, Whittingehame
Tower, East Lothian

BELOW: 86. Common walnut,
Stirling Castle

ABOVE: 88. Black mulberry,
Luffness, Aberlady, East
Lothian

90. Oriental plane,
Tyninghame walled garden,
East Lothian

91. Eugene's poplar, Royal
Botanic Garden Edinburgh
(felled 2001)

BELOW: 92. Chinese
necklace poplar, Brodick
Castle, Isle of Arran

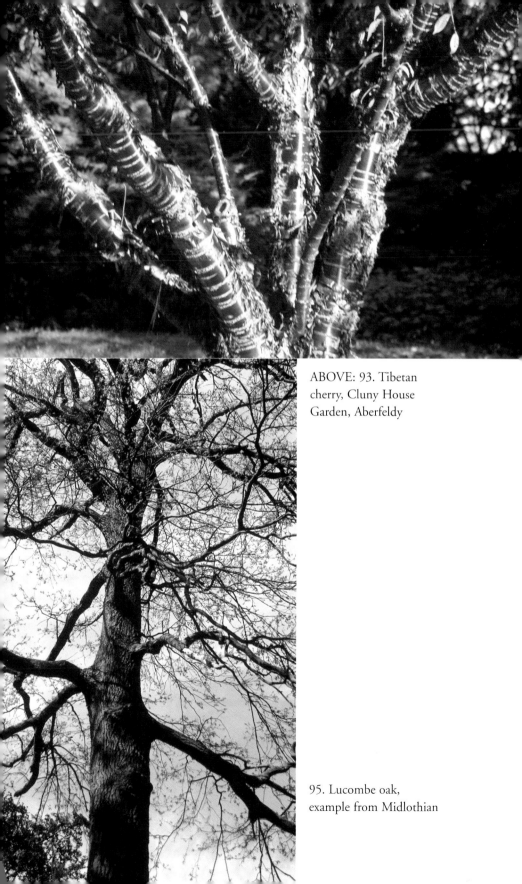

ABOVE: 93. Tibetan
cherry, Cluny House
Garden, Aberfeldy

95. Lucombe oak,
example from Midlothian

ABOVE: 97. Small leaved lime,
Arniston, Gorebridge, Midlothian

100. *Zelkova verschaffeltii*,
Crathes, by Banchory

Conversely, they do not live long compared with other pines – 60 years is not unusual. The Cairnsmore tree is just about as perfect as it is possible to imagine; always having had uninterrupted growing space, never, surprisingly, having been torn about by the gales, and growing in distinguished company. Hasten along before it is too late and thank the Champion family who put it there.

61. AUSTRIAN PINE *PINUS NIGRA VAR. NIGRA*
DAWYCK BOTANIC GARDEN, STOBO, PEEBLES-SHIRE
Royal Botanic Garden Edinburgh
Opening hours
(See second photo section)

All that you need to produce a second Dawyck is three and a bit centuries, the knowledge, commitment and wealth of at least five generations in three families and the Royal Botanic Garden happy to accept the place as a gift when the private will gave up. I don't know of a parallel example in Scotland.

Dawyck is less than an hour away from my home and a constant attraction in all seasons. Here are the first Scottish European silver firs planted in 1680 by the Veitchs, whose descendants became famous nurserymen. Here are amongst the first European larch to be planted in Scotland, in 1725, by Sir James Naesmyth or Naysmith. Here are some of the original Wellingtonias and Douglas firs planted by Sir James's son John, and the fastigiate 'Dawyck' beech that he found as a stray seedling in the woods. Here is the first Brewer's spruce in Britain, brought back from the Siskiyou Mountains in 1906 by the energetic and well-informed F.G.S. Balfour. Dawyck lost 50,000 trees in the gale of 14–15 January 1968. The RBGE took over in 1978. David Knott, the present curator, is fully conscious and capable of his place in this line of descent.

Of all the fine trees at Dawyck the pines are particularly pleasing, tall, healthy and well presented. On Policy Bank below the Beech Walk are as good-looking ponderosa, Macedonian, Korean and Digger pines as you will see anywhere, keeping excellent company with this, the first Austrian pine planted in Britain and, at 134 ft high and 11 ft girth, the largest.

The tree was grown from the first batch of seed introduced by Lawson, Nurseryman of Edinburgh in 1835. It is usually assigned a planting date of 1840. Sir John Naysmith, who planted it, says 1836–37. It is not unusual for a tree to be five or more years from seed before being planted in its final station, so both may be right.

In Scotland, Austrian pine is a coarse tree compared with its first cousin, the Corsican pine. It has generally been used as shelter, for which it is excellent, not least in such polluted atmospheres as Auld Reekie until a few decades ago. The timber is generally dismissed as worthless, which is true enough for us but you would not say that of some of the majestic stands in its natural heartlands – parts of Italy, Austria, Hungary, the former Yugoslavia, Albania and Greece.

62. MACEDONIAN PINE *PINUS PEUCE*
ARDTORNISH ESTATE, MORVEN
Mrs Faith Raven
Open

Perhaps the Macedonian pine would be better known if the botanical name was easier to pronounce. Uninhibited foresters call it 'puke-ay'; the more abashed soften the 'c' to 'puch-ay'. Allen Coombes says 'poy-kay'. The infallible, classically trained H. Gibert-Carter prints the Greek, saying that it is the name of a resinous tree in Theophrastus. Not having Greek characters to hand, I must spell it out as 'Pi, epsilon, hypsilon, kappa, eta' and leave the pronunciation to others.

By any name the Macedonian pine is, almost invariably, an enjoyable tree, neat, regular, bright green, the picture of health, with a characteristic columnar shape. It grows not only regularly but at a very reasonable rate. I have seldom seen a poor one. There are two trees on Policy Bank at Dawyck that I particularly admire but I have decided to talk about Ardtornish for two reasons. First, we are very fond of the place, taking all the grandchildren there each autumn. Second, unusually and possibly uniquely, the three Ardtornish trees are producing seedlings, and one in particular is surrounded by healthy and happy regeneration mostly from knee-high to ankle-high. It is just over 9 ft in girth and I suppose may be 80 or 90 years old. There is, as you might guess, an expensive, effective deer fence round the whole wooded garden, making possible not only the growth of these sapling pines but many other good and unexpected things. There is something particularly satisfying about an introduced tree that will regenerate naturally unless it is over-productive or in the wrong place.

The Macedonian pine is a native of the mountains of Albania, the former Yugoslavia, Bulgaria and Macedonia. It was not 'discovered', surprisingly, until 1839 nor introduced to the western European market until 1863. There are only two five-needled pines in Europe, this and the arolla pine.

The Macedonian pine apart, my favourite tree at Ardtornish is a silver lime between the estate yard and the footbridge into the policies proper. It is not so much a tree as an elongated bush of vigorous upright stems. It took longer than I care to remember for the penny to drop about the reason for this strange growth pattern. These are the now vertical branches of a fallen lime, the former trunk of which has rotted away or been covered by alluvium brought down by the burn.

63. TOTARA *PODOCARPUS TOTARA*
INVEREWE GARDENS, POOLEWE
The National Trust for Scotland
Opening hours

Osgood Mackenzie started planting on the treeless peninsula of Inverewe in 1865 using, in his own words, 'Endless cartloads of peaty stuff from old turf dykes, red soil carted long distances and a kind of blue clay marl from below the sea, full of decayed oyster shells and crabs

and other good things, hauled up at very low tides.' By 1907, under the shelter then established, he was able to show the great W.J. Bean, among other things, *Tricuspidarias, Embothriums, Eucryphias, Eucalypts, Acacia dealbata* and this *Podocarp*, which, though significantly reduced in area, remains one of the great trees and most valuable timbers of New Zealand.

Thanks to Osgood until his death in 1922, to his daughter Mairi Sawyer until 1952, when she gifted Inverewe to the NTS with an endowment, to their gardeners Donald Grant, Kenneth John Urquhart and Murdo Cameron, and to the succession of NTS plantsmen, including Dr John Cowan, Professor Henderson, Dick Fulcher, Peter Clough and now Simon McPhun, Inverewe is one of the essential Scottish gardens to know, to visit, to exist.

The trees which, as shelter, have best withstood the tests of more than a century of Scottish weather have been predominantly Scots pine with larch, beech, alder and eucalypts from the Tasmanian mountains. On a lesser scale, but just as interesting, are those of the world's pines best adapted to maritime conditions such as Corsican pine, and the row of Bishop pine in the car park which come from the coast of California.

Within the shelter there are continuously trees to catch the eye and the imagination: the mottled trunk of an enormous snow gum, say, or a huge Campbell's magnolia or the cinnamon, velvety bark of a Chilean myrtle. Totara has its place in this distinguished company.

You will not see many of the world's hundred or so species of podocarp anywhere in Britain and there are only three capable of exceeding 60 ft – two from Chile and this New Zealander. The best are all along the mild west coast. They are conifers, near relatives of the yew. This Inverewe totara (there is a second) looks entirely happy and, at 4 ft girth, not insubstantial. The leaves are evergreen, linear and leathery, with a sharp point. The bark is gloriously shaggy. It is a bit short though of a tree called Pouakani in the Pureora Forest Reserve, west of Lake Taupo in North Island, New Zealand. Pouakani is 180 ft high with a girth of 38 ft and is said, though on what authority I do not know, to be 1,800 years old.

The Maoris prized the giant totara, a tree for every purpose, notably using it for ceremonial buildings and their great war-canoes. The wood is durable in the ground and fine-grained, just right for carving.

64. DOUGLAS FIR *PSEUDOTSUGA MENZIESII*
DRUMLANRIG, DUMFRIESSHIRE
The Duke of Buccleuch
Opening hours

Our host one year in Bavaria was repairing the barn built by his grandfather with timber cut from the well-managed and beautiful local forests whence the original timbers had come. They are not natural forests in the strict sense but they contain the tree species they have always contained and they are managed, largely through natural regeneration, on a silviculture already settled by the seventeenth century.

Contrast that with our own situation. We removed most of our indigenous forest several millennia ago. Whenever we have needed timber in quantity, we have imported it from the countries round the Baltic, from Canada or from the tropical forests of an erstwhile empire. The turning point came, as did so much else, during the First World War. The vision that we could and should grow our own timber had complex origins, but a fact central to that vision was the performance in numerous arboreta up and down the country of conifers brought here from the Pacific coast of North America. The two of crucial importance, Sitka spruce and Douglas fir, were among the 210 new species collected and introduced by the tireless and fearless David Douglas, born in 1799, the son of a Perthshire stonemason. Do read the biography by Ann Lindsay Mitchell and Syd House written for the bi-centenary. I have thought that, born later, David Douglas might have played rugby scrum-half for Scotland in the mould of Roy Armstrong or Gary Armstrong – tough, fearless and determined.

Of all the introduced conifers the Douglas fir has always been my favourite. (It is not a true fir, but the cones are so distinctive and constant that there should be no difficulties in identification.) It is a beautiful and distinguished tree in youth and old age. It is a strong, distinctive, attractive timber, still the mainstay of the lumber industry of the North American west coast. We panelled one wall of our Elgin kitchen with Douglas fir cut from Monaughty Forest, ten miles to the west, and milled by Riddochs of Rothiemay at Mosstodloch, ten miles to the east. Very satisfying – on the Bavarian model.

Every forester in Scotland has a favourite Douglas fir or, more usually, a Douglas fir stand. You will find passionate advocates of the Hermitage, Murthly, Moniack or Reelig Glen, Buchanty Spout, Barcaldine or Dunans at Glendaruel. There are so many big trees to choose from. Perhaps a score are now over 200 ft and there are many youngsters coming up to take their place.

The tree at Drumlanrig is very fine but it owes its place here to the human story behind it. Not only is it from the original 1827 seed lot but it was also a gift from David Douglas to his brother, then working on the estate.

65. UMBRELLA PINE *SCIADOPITYS VERTICILLATA*
ARMADALE CASTLE, ISLE OF SKYE
The Clan Donald Centre Trust
Opening hours

The first umbrella pine that I remember seeing was in the Quarry Gardens at Gordon Castle, Fochabers, a 40 ft, neat, dense, triangular tree with distinctive whorls of thick glossy needles. I was right to think it distinctive. It is a genus of a single species. There is nothing else like it anywhere in the world.

The umbrella pine grows naturally only on mountains in Japan, usually in mixed woods. It was known to European collectors by 1775 but seed only reached the west in 1861, thanks to Robert Fortune and J.G. Veitch. Few were planted before 1910. Japanese trees are said to exceed 100 ft. There is one tree in Kent approaching 80 ft. With us, 40 or 50 ft is good going.

On the strength of the Gordon Castle tree, I began by thinking of umbrella pine as a rare exotic, probably difficult to cultivate. The next one I saw, however, was in a small front garden in Inverurie, surrounded by cheerful annuals. In the many ensuing years I have met them frequently, almost always solitary and often tucked away as though the planter was not too sure about the effect. Yet they are neat, healthy and fairly vigorous. It would be pleasant to make a bolder statement with this idiosyncratic tree, a grove at least as at Kilmun or, better, a quincunx.

Many people ask how I know where to find a particular tree. The answer is often that I stumble across it or that Alan Mitchell measured it and noted the fact in one of his books and articles. Both were true of the umbrella pine at Armadale. This was one of the best examples in Scotland, with a height of 40 ft until the top was badly damaged in gales during January 1984. About half the crown was lost when one of the two leading stems snapped. The damage was compounded in the autumn gales of 1988. It is reckoned, at 6 ft, to have the largest girth in Britain.

In 1989 the Japanese Ambassador of the day, His Excellency Kazuo Chiba, planted the first of a number of successors at Armadale. All are growing well.

There are cones on most of the trees I know. In my experience the seed germinates readily though, curiously, I have never seen a natural seedling. For the first few years, growth is startlingly slow. Once growing, 1 ft per year is quite normal.

66. GIANT SEQUOIA *SEQUOIADENDRON GIGANTEUM*
CASTLE LEOD, STRATHPEFFER
The Earl of Cromartie
Private but may visit with permission

There is a constant and forgivable confusion between this tree and the coast redwood or *Sequoia sempervirens*. Perhaps the most pleasant route to sorting them out is to take tea at Kinfauns Castle Hotel just east of Perth, where, from the tall windows, you will see a matched pair, each more than 130 ft tall. For good measure, in the foreground, there is probably the best swamp cypress in Scotland, a tree with which the coast redwood was initially confused.

At home, which is only in California, there is no scope for confusion. The coast redwood grows in more or less pure stands only in the fog belt, no more than 50 km from the Pacific. The giant sequoia grows in about 80 groves in mixture with firs and pines, between 1,800 and 2,400 m, on the western slopes of the Sierras with deep snow in winter and virtually no summer rainfall.

Coast redwood is the tallest tree in the world at 373 ft. The girth of the tallest tree is 43 ft. The giant sequoia called 'General Sherman' in the Sequoia National Park is the largest living thing on earth, having a girth of 80 ft and a height of 290 ft. The age is estimated at anything between 2,700 and 3,500 years old. No wonder Americans become restive if they hear their tree called Wellingtonia after the Great Duke.

As I write there is no giant sequoia in Scotland older than 148 years and no coast redwood older than 157 years. In point of height growth our youngsters are already impressive. The giant sequoia at Castle Leod is, at 180 ft, the tallest in Britain, probably in Europe and possibly anywhere in the world outside California. Strathpeffer is almost exactly 20 degrees north of the most northerly stand in California. In point of girth the largest sequoia in Scotland is at Cluny House, near Aberfeldy.

Very few Scottish sequoias are struck by lightning, which is a frequent occurrence in England. They never blow over unless their roots are

maltreated. Given a reasonable rainfall they are as well furnished as you could wish.

When seed became available in 1853, it was in large quantities. Within a decade or so there was scarcely an estate without a sequoia or several, frequently in avenues. I find the 14-tree avenue at Benmore, in moist Argyll, entirely appropriate. I am not so comfortable with the isolated crescent at the House of Dun (NTS) in Angus. Too many have lost their tops. They look a little pinched and uneasy in contrast to the elegant symmetries of the house by William Adam.

The Castle Leod tree is a perfect, healthy spire, an appropriate foil to the castle and to the remarkable 1550 sweet chestnut in the park below.

67. SWAMP CYPRESS *TAXODIUM DISTICHUM*
BARGANY ESTATE, BY GIRVAN
Mr N.J.F. Dalrymple-Hamilton
Open March to October
(See second photo section)

There are bigger swamp cypress in Scotland, but none that I know better placed than this pair at Bargany. They stand on a mini-island within a small dark loch, enlivened with water lilies. The loch is surrounded and overhung by substantial oaks, beeches, horse chestnuts, and limes intermingled with pines, firs, sequoias, Japanese cedars and an enormous Sitka spruce. In late May the whole surround and the island explode with the colours and the heady scent of azaleas and rhododendrons. The dominant unifying colour is bold yellow but the grace notes are orange, white, pink, purple and a vivid blue. This is the moment too of maximum birdsong. When I was there a Garden Warbler was in vigorous competition with a Blackbird.

Swamp cypresses come from the south-eastern and southern coasts of the USA and the river valleys that drain into them. Unsurprisingly, they grow best in Britain in the warmer south, in well-watered gardens along the Thames for example. It is a little surprising that they make any headway in Scotland but there is a very fine tree in the garden of Kinfauns, now a hotel, east of Perth and another in the damp ground near the pond at the RBGE.

Bargany lost many trees, as did Culzean Castle just down the way, in the Boxing Day gale of 1998 but a good number of the trees described in the entertaining booklet, written and illustrated by Lady Dalrymple-Hamilton, mother of the present laird, have survived, including these swamp cypress.

The public is welcome. When I was there the dog belonging to a local family was in disgrace, having wallowed in the mud around the pond before going for a swim among the water lilies. It looked like fun.

68. CLIPPED YEW *TAXUS BACCATA*
MEGGINCH CASTLE, ERROL, PERTHSHIRE
Captain Drummond of Megginch and Baroness Strange
Opening hours

There is nothing, unless it is the monkey puzzle, which has divided aesthetic opinion quite like topiary. Do you detest 'Nature subdued by Art'?

Topiary, the art of clipping yew, holly, box, even rosemary into unnatural shapes, has its roots in Rome. Read Pliny the Younger. There were successive waves of enthusiasm for the practice in the fourteenth century, on the return of Charles II from his enforced experience of Versailles and Le Nôtre, and on the arrival of William and Mary, who set about creating gardens in the Dutch style at Hampton Court and Kensington Palace. The intent was to establish 'those Symetrys which silently express a reigning Order, Peace, Harmony and Beauty'.

The reaction came in the reign of Queen Anne, helped along by the wit of Addison and Pope. This is the 6th Earl of Haddington in 1734, forthright as ever:

. . . for these Fifty Years past the Clipping [of yews] and I think

spoiling them has been the Practice. I have now cut all the
Featherings off my Yews, and reduced them to Single Stems.
How they'll Succeed I can not tell, but I shall never try to put
any Ever Green in a shape but its own, unless in a hedge.

Tastes change. Drummond Castle was redesigned around 1832. The
elaborate topiary at Fingask, on the slope to the north of the Carse of
Gowrie, was created between 1850 and 1882. The crown made of
golden and green yews at Megginch, depicted above, was created to
celebrate the jubilee of Queen Victoria in 1887.

What I want to celebrate is not only topiary in an exact sense but big,
clipped yews. (They are the same species as the unclipped yews of
churchyards.) Many of them, most of them perhaps, are overgrown

hedges, yews that had an exuberant period out of control before being taken back in hand. I think of the rolling, elephantine yews at Crathes or Luffness at Aberlady, or Drummond, or Megginch itself. They are more than hedges, less than shelter-belts and of great practical value in a windy country. I also think of the quartet of yews at Malleny, Balerno, each like a huge, green, lawyer's wig mushroom.

69. WESTERN HEMLOCK *TSUGA HETEROPHYLLA*
LENY HOUSE, CALLANDER
Mr and Mrs A.F. Roebuck
A private hotel but owners very welcoming (visible from the access road)

David Douglas spent many days in the west, below or beside or overlooking this the western hemlock, but, apparently, did not recognise it as different from the hemlock he knew from eastern America. Whatever the reason he did not send home seed and it was not until 1862, more than 30 years later, that this handsome tree became available in quantity here.

It did not help the progress of the tree in Scottish forestry that it was derided as a weed-tree by American loggers. That reputation was demonstrated to be wrong, but not until the Second World War. Here, as at home, it is a perfectly acceptable general purpose softwood – pale brown, fine-grained and easily worked. There is simply not enough of it, given the present technology, for sawmillers to market it separately.

Utility aside, western hemlock is among the most beautiful of conifers added to our landscape, almost invariably well furnished and vigorous. Given its native distribution in the fog belt of the American west coast, it is unsurprising that the best growth with us is also in the humid west though it is very happy in Perthshire and very reasonable in the east if not too exposed – at Yester, East Lothian, for example. The leading shoot always hangs over in a graceful crook, the branches always droop and the foliage is friendly to push through.

After a decade or two of growth you will need a torch to see your way under a stand of hemlock since it casts a shade as deep as any tree we grow except beech, yew and some of the silver firs. These are the species to grow if you have to shade out the invasive *Rhododendron ponticum.*

Hemlock is very willing to regenerate from seed. In due course it can make a major contribution to the increasing number of uneven-aged, continuous cover forests.

Everyone with an eye for trees will have a favourite hemlock or stand of hemlocks. For me it is the extraordinarily narrow, shapely spire, now something like 160 ft high, which grows out of the dell below Leny House. You can glimpse the tree as you drive towards Callander from the Falls of Leny. You will be a lot safer turning up the access road to Leny House to get a proper view.

PARTICULAR BROADLEAVES

70. OREGON MAPLE *ACER MACROPHYLLUM*
KILMUN ARBORETUM, NEAR DUNOON, ARGYLL
Forest Enterprise
Open

Kilmun is just up the road from Dunoon, ten minutes from the Younger Botanic Garden. It is open all year long, free, laced with footpaths, beautiful and unique in Scotland because you can see 162 tree species planted here, not as individuals but as groups or mini-forests. You are not looking at *a* monkey puzzle, say, or *a* Japanese cedar, or *a* mountain hemlock, but at groves of these remarkable trees drawn in from all the world. I went round last with a friend who had never seen the like. He was laughing with pleasure.

Kilmun has been on the go for 70 years but outside the specialist forestry publications you will be hard pressed to find any mention of it, let alone a detailed guidebook. Labels used to be meticulous; now half are missing. Forest Enterprise is searching for a future purpose, perhaps as a site for conserving some of the world's endangered conifers. But what is there already is priceless. We need some new designation, something like National Heritage Wood, to point up the value and to underpin the funding.

Unsurprisingly, given the research origins and climate of Kilmun, the accent is on conifers, but there are 42 broadleaves here, none more interesting than the Oregon maple. The name is something of a misnomer since it ranges from Alaska to California, although it is certainly at its majestic best around Puget Sound and the lower Columbia River. It grows from the coast into the foothills both as an associate of the huge firs and spruces and along roads and as farm lots. Under ideal conditions it becomes an enormous tree – 150 ft has been recorded. The leaves are the largest of any maple but so dissected that they are always airy and on such long stalks that they are never still.

With us it is fully hardy. There are big trees at Newbattle Abbey, Dalkeith, in the RBGE and at Brodick on Arran but surprisingly few elsewhere. Since Oregon maple grows twice as fast as the native oaks and makes fine timber why should it not become a forest tree in its own right? It would also be the perfect understorey (beneath the canopy of the dominant trees) to make a plantation of Sitka spruce or Douglas fir look like and feel like a forest.

71. ITALIAN MAPLE *ACER OPALUS*
GLASGOW BOTANIC GARDENS, GREAT WESTERN ROAD
City of Glasgow Council
Opening hours

It is curious how the mind works. What I remember about the Glasgow Botanic Gardens is that the indefatigable Sir William Hooker, later the first director of Kew, was instrumental in the development of the collection while Regius Professor of Botany in the city, that David Douglas worked in the gardens, that Gladstone and Disraeli addressed at length the masses assembled in the Kibble Palace and that up by the flagstaff there is a shapely example of this largish-growing maple, not often seen in Scotland. I have to look up the books to remind myself that Hooker was Professor for the 20 years 1821–41, that Douglas trained on the earlier site for the three years between 1820 and 1823 and that the gardens were moved to this site from Sandyford by 1842.

Acer opalus is a mountain tree of the western Mediterranean and southern Alps extending northwards to the Jura. It is to be found fairly frequently in central European parks but very seldom in Britain. Leaf size and shape, and stature are very variable, something between field maple and sycamore, so that the tree is rather easy to miss, unless in autumnal yellow or in March and April, when the hanging yellow flowers precede the leaves to give the whole broad crown a luminosity unequalled at this time of year. Given the success of this Glasgow tree and the two at Smeaton Hepburn, East Lothian, which are the largest in Britain, it is disappointing that we do not see it more often.

H. Gilbert-Carter tells us that *opalus* means opal. With characteristic certainty, he goes on, 'the word intended must be *opulus*, the name of a tree in Pliny'.

There are many other well-grown, unusual trees in these gardens, notably a Himalayan birch, a Chinese cedar, an Amur cork tree and a particularly fine black oak, *Quercus velutina*.

Incidentally, the Royal Botanic Garden Edinburgh is insistently singular while the Glasgow Gardens are contentedly plural. Is there some subtle Glasgow/Edinburgh divide here that I am not grasping?

72. NORWAY MAPLE *ACER PLATANOIDES*
CASTLE FRASER, KEMNAY, ABERDEENSHIRE
The National Trust for Scotland
Opening hours

Not having been there I cannot say whether the Taj Mahal at midnight lives up to its reputation. I can assert, however, that the New England fall surpassed our high expectations. We had borrowed a friend's house in backwoods Vermont (not that there is much other than backwoods in Vermont) and had the surrounding trees and woods to watch as they went through their dazzling changes. Many of the tree species were familiar from arboreta in Britain but we could now see them growing in their natural context.

The fall does not happen to us in Britain, or at least does not happen

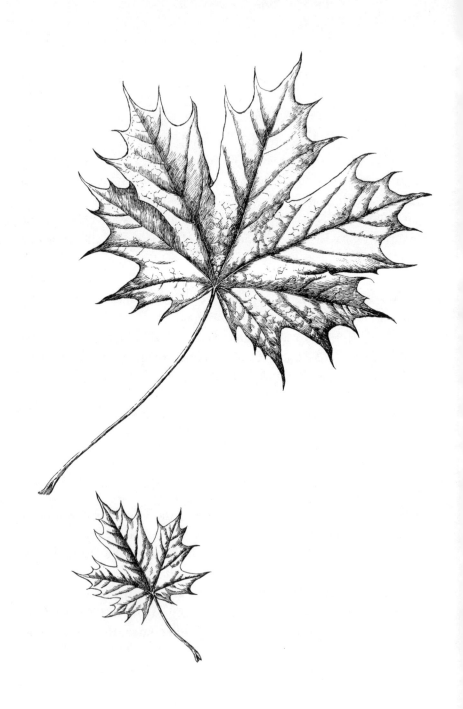

to anything like the same degree as in New England, for good reasons. Essentially, we have an oceanic climate while they have a continental climate. It therefore does not often help to grow the classic New England trees in Scotland. I live near a red maple that quietly drops its leaves one day in early November, without great effect. The few sugar maples you encounter in Scotland, including a biggish tree in the Stornoway Lews Castle woods, are not much more accommodating. Usually the best display from eastern American trees is from what we call the American red oak. It grows here with such surprising vigour that foresters have occasionally planted it in hectares. You do not often meet its cousin, the scarlet oak, in this country but when you do, at Doune House for example, Innes House in Moray or Lennoxlove outside Haddington or, a superb tree at Kippenross near Dunblane, you wonder if they might not be more widely planted in those parts of inland Scotland where the autumn temperatures most nearly mimic those of New England.

The best of our largish, native, or near native, trees for autumn colour are beech, birch, field maple, oak, grey poplar, crack willow and gean. They are all in the yellow-orange-brown spectrum. Ash is a clearer yellow. Best of all the yellows is aspen, flaring and unmistakable, often way up on the hill beside a burn. For policy woods, parklands and imaginative townscapes, there could be added the raoul and roble beech from South America and silver pendent lime, Caucasian wingnut and Caucasian zelkova. For depth and vibrancy of autumn colour I put my money on the European larch. For the most reliable and vivid red there is nothing better than Sargent's cherry.

There can be a little confusion between Norway maple and sycamore. Both can grow into big trees in Scotland, as elsewhere. The differences in bark, flowering and leaf detail are, however, marked. Norway maple has a smooth bark, the yellow flowers grow at the ends of the shoots and the lobes of the leaves are drawn out to a point. It used to be tapped for its sweet sap, like the Canadian sugar maple, a feature that you can check by breaking a leaf stalk across. The natural distribution of Norway maple is eastwards from southern Scandinavia to the Caucasus. It has also been widely planted in western Europe for its conspicuous flowers and reliable autumn colours.

This tree at Castle Fraser is thoroughly representative of the species and, with a girth of 12 ft, as large as any in Scotland. I do not know the age but would guess that it may not be more than 150 years old. Norway maple is, sensibly, the preferred replacement tree for the city elms of Edinburgh's parks and drives. It has been used extensively along new roads, though you do not notice it until the leaves begin to turn, often red to begin with, then yellow or brown.

73. SYCAMORE OR GREAT PLANE *ACER PSEUDOPLATANUS*
THE HIRSEL, COLDSTREAM
The Earl of Hume
Open in 'reasonable daylight hours' throughout the year

Many of the largest, presumed oldest, sycamores in Britain can be found within 100 miles of Edinburgh. There is no agreement as to why this might be but the Auld Alliance between Scotland and France, one of the natural homes of sycamore, may have had something to do with it. The oldest tree with a reasonably reliable planting date, 1550, is at Newbattle Abbey, Dalkeith. There is a 1901 full-plate photograph of the tree in its prime, in Elwes and Henry, but it has been 'going back', as foresters say, for half a century. The largest sycamore in Scotland, except perhaps the superb tree on the edge of the Tay behind Birnam, is in the park at Tyninghame. It is 25 ft in girth. It has begun to show the first thinning in the crown. There are healthy trees with girths of between 20 and 22 ft at, for example, Ford by Telford's great bridge north of Pathhead, Midlothian, Posso up the Manor Water above Peebles, Drumlanrig in Dumfriesshire, Kippenross near Dunblane, Yester in East Lothian and Newliston in West Lothian. There are none better presented than this fully crowned, rudely vigorous specimen just outside the walled garden at The Hirsel.

There is a local legend that it was planted to commemorate Flodden in 1513. That seems an inherently unlikely response to such a monumental disaster. Moreover, 487 years would be a very unusual age for a sycamore still, as this is, in unblemished health. What is certain, however, is that the great plane or sycamore was well established as an introduced species in Scotland before Flodden. For example a tree at Kippenross measured in 1798 was 22.5 ft in girth, suggesting an origin before 1400. 'A favourite Scotch tree,' says Sir Thomas Dick Lauder in 1834, unembarrassed by the adjective. A century earlier, in 1735, the 6th Earl of Haddington wrote:

> I believe this is what in England, goes by the Name of the Sycamore. By what I can Observe, this seems to have been the Favourite Tree in all the north part of Britain, for there is no Old Seat, no Gentleman's house, nor any place where Old Trees are, but the Plains, are the most numerous.

As well they might be. For a continental tree it has grown spectacularly well from Shetland to the Mull of Galloway, from 500m up the hill to within salt-splash at the coast. It regenerates in profusion. Sycamore is clearly inappropriate in reserves set aside to conserve native woodland, in small gardens or other confined spaces. Where there is room for a huge tree, however, this is an excellent choice: easy, hardy, long-lived, improving with age and a splendid timber. Whether it is 'rich in wildlife', depends on your definition of rich and wildlife. Perhaps 'Scotch maple' would be an apt name for a tree that lives so long and appears so comfortable here.

74. THE CORSTORPHINE SYCAMORE
ACER PSEUDOPLATANUS 'CORSTORPHINENSE'
CORSTORPHINE, EDINBURGH
The Corstorphine Trust
Visible from the street
(See second photo section)

The entire crown of the Corstorphine Sycamore was torn off by the gale on the night of 26 December 1998. On Blackford Hill, not far away, the maximum wind speed that night was measured as 107 mph. The tree was approaching its 400th birthday, the sole survivor of an avenue planted probably by Hugh Forrester. At the end it was nearly 15 ft in girth, having been 11 ft in 1880, as measured by the accurate Robert Hutchison.

What made the Corstorphine Sycamore unique was its unfurling leaves. In the words of the 1795 Statistical Account, 'In the end of May and the beginning of June, [it] exhibits an appearance of the most striking beauty . . . the colour of the leaves is the richest vivid yellow hue.' By mid-July the leaves were a standard dark green, indistinguishable from other sycamores.

I write as though that was that. In fact the Corstorphine Sycamore has been massively propagated over the years and may be encountered in all manner of likely and unlikely places. As with Dolly the sheep, all are genetically identical. The Corstorphine Trust, to whom the tree was gifted by William Dickson, the last Dickson laird of Corstorphine, has planted a replacement on the site, which is in an enclosure but visible from the street. The Trust had made and sold numbers of very pleasant bowls turned from the fallen wood.

Not only was the Corstorphine Sycamore botanically unique, it was also the scene of a murder that took place on 26 August 1679. James Baillie, second Lord Forrester, was murdered by Mrs Christian Nimmo, née Hamilton. She was his deceased wife's niece and, allegedly, his mistress. He had come from the local hostelry. She was waiting for him at the tree. There was a violent quarrel. She killed him with his own sword and, in due course, was executed.

75. MADRONA *ARBUTUS MENZIESII*
CASTLE MENZIES, WEEM, BY ABERFELDY
The Clan Menzies Society
Open
(See second photo section)

Once seen, never forgotten – the trunk of a maturing Madrona. There is nothing like it other than some of the tall rhododendrons. Think of brick-red, subdued orange and quiet green, in complex combinations, on a smooth, strokeable surface.

The first Madrona I saw was a handsome tree planted in 1932 at Innes House in Moray. The second was this equally robust, equally healthy tree at, appropriately, Castle Menzies. It was planted about 1870 as part of the arboretum established by Sir Robert Menzies (1844–1903), from seed collected by Jeffrey, Browne and others in California and British Columbia. Thereafter I have enjoyed trees of between 35 and 45 ft at Crathes on Deeside, Crarae in Argyll, Marchmont near Greenlaw, the RBGE and, the biggest, at Carberry Tower, near Musselburgh. So I do get a little jumpy when I read, in more than one account, that the Madrona does not grow in Scotland. It would be strange if it did not, given a natural distribution up the west coast of North America from California to British Columbia either as a tallish constituent of the coastal forests or a near shrub in the mountains. This area has a similar climate to Scotland and trees from there do particularly well with us.

In their early years, Madronas require a dry root zone and some protection from cold wind and frost. A number from Californian seed germinated at Glendoick and planted under dappled shade are forming their first flowers after about 25 years. Foresters are very conscious of the influence of provenance on the performance of north-west American trees in Scotland. A priori, we would be looking to Washington or British Columbia for the best fit.

'This is,' says Bean, 'one of the most beautiful of all broadleaved trees,' adding a quotation that, 'the traveller, forester, hunter, artist, and botanist is held by the spell of its crown of flowers, and masses of red fruit, its terracotta bark and burnished foliage.' It is an evergreen, a member of the heather family and first cousin of the strawberry tree that grows naturally in Killarney.

Arbutus Menziesii was described by and named after Archibald Menzies (1754–1842), naval surgeon and botanist with the Vancouver expedition, and was introduced by David Douglas.

76. SPANISH CHESTNUT *CASTANEA SATIVA*
BALMERINO ABBEY, FIFE
The National Trust for Scotland
Open
(See second photo section for example at Melville Castle)

Given that the natural distribution of the Spanish or sweet chestnut is probably all south of the Alps, it grows remarkably well and old in Scotland. Its average lifespan is perhaps third longest after yew and oak, and ahead, though not by much, of sycamore and common lime.

The oldest dated chestnut in Scotland is the very remarkable tree at Castle Leod outside Strathpeffer, planted in 1550. There are trees almost as big but undated at Newbattle Abbey and Melville Castle, both near Dalkeith. The latter is known, perversely, as Rizzio's or Riccio's oak. It seems exceptionally unlikely that Rizzio took time out for a spot of tree planting, but the dates fit and you never know . . .

There is a legend that this redoubtable chestnut at Balmerino Abbey was planted by Queen Ermengarda, wife of William the Lion, who founded the Abbey in the twelfth century. The NTS has spoilt this speculation by demonstrating that it dates from the mid-sixteenth century and thus is of an age with the Castle Leod tree.

Because the bole is leaning and there are huge horizontal boughs, the tree is strictly immeasurable but you can think of it as being about 20 ft round.

Chestnuts are produced in Scotland but they are poor things compared to the 'marrons' of the Mediterranean or even of southern England. The wood is a little like oak in appearance but softer and easier to carve. In larger dimensions it is liable to split and cup. So we must think of chestnut in the north as a long-lived, ornamental tree, full of character in youth and age.

The Balmerino tree has been patched with concrete and propped on metal supports. Arboricultural opinion no longer favours such treatments, preferring to let wind and weather take their natural course to the benefit of ecology and aesthetics.

77. KATSURA *CERCIDIPHYLLUM JAPONICUM*
BATTLEBY, REDGORTON, PERTHSHIRE
Scottish Natural Heritage
Access with permission
(see second photo section)

There are few substantial Scottish gardens without this tree. At home in Japan and western China, it is one of the largest broadleaves, some say the largest, reaching heights of 130 ft and girths of 18 ft. It is probable that such dimensions will be achieved in the United States. With us, the tallest are approaching 60 ft and girths of 6 ft without any noticeable geographical bias. The main hazard is late spring frosts. New leaves can be wiped out in a night, though they always seem to grow again.

There is a shock of pleasure when encountering a katsura. The leaves are elegantly rounded, curiously arranged and in October turn yellow, orange or red or combinations of all three. The winter tracery is distinctive: very regularly spaced pairs of neat opposite buds. As the leaves fall, there is the remarkable, unique, powerful smell of burnt sugar.

The fine katsuras at Battleby are said to be the first 14 planted in Scotland, probably in the first decade of last century. Battleby was the headquarters of the Countryside Commission from 1970 until the shotgun marriage with the NCC on 1 April 1991. It is now an arm of the SNH headquarters. Anyone visiting the Battleby centre is welcome to look around the estate, as are casual strangers, but everyone should ask permission.

Katsuras aside, there is much to enjoy at Battleby. Sir Alexander Cross built up the collection while he leased the property from shortly after the First World War, eventually buying it in 1947. The Countryside Commission looked after and added to the collection. Do not miss the Big Wood to the north of the house. The well-spaced oaks, with a surprising understorey of rhododendrons and umbrella pines, are some of the best sessile oaks that I know anywhere. There is also an excellent mountain hemlock, two shapely Nikko maples, a trio of Turkey oaks as you approach the house and an isolated 80 ft silver birch to remind you of how handsome this native can be in a designed space.

78. BENTHAM'S CORNEL *CORNUS CAPITATA*
TOROSAY CASTLE, ISLE OF MULL
Mr Christopher James
Opening hours

Until this year I would have said that Bentham's cornel did not grow in Scotland. Too cold, I would have said, for an evergreen broadleaf from the Himalayas. I was wrong and for the same reason as Dr Samuel Johnson gave the lady: 'Sheer ignorance, Madam.' There is an entirely splendid tree at Torosay Castle, near the Craignure ferry terminal on Mull. It is bigger than any outside Cornwall or Southern Ireland, 44 ft high and almost as wide. There are two seasons to see the tree at its best. At midsummer, when it is covered with what appear to be pale-yellow flowers but are actually bracts surrounding the clustered flowers, and from late October to early November when the flowers give rise to crimson fruit, 3 cm across, not unlike strawberries. You have to look sharpish though because they are quickly eaten by thrushes and blackbirds, despite the insecure footholds.

Mike Swift, who is head gardener at Torosay, tells me that the tree was planted in about 1935 and speculates that it may have come from lower elevations in Yunnan. His wife Jenny says it is not difficult to propagate from seed, though the seedlings are vulnerable to voles. Not one of the three of us knows whether the fruit is 'edible and good', like *Cornus kousa* which comes from further east.

A distinctive feature of the cornels and dogwoods is that the leaf veins run parallel to the leaf margins; that is, they are closer to the midrib at either end than in the middle. A pleasant feature is that, if you gently break the leaf across, the two bits will remain connected by the elasticated vascular bundles. Try it. Astonish your friends.

The Bentham from whom the tree gets its name was George Bentham (1800–84), a distinguished and prolific English botanist. The Latin *capitata* means 'growing in a dense head', an apt description of the fruit.

79. TABLE DOGWOOD *CORNUS CONTROVERSA* '*VARIEGATA*'
BROUGHTON HOUSE, KIRKCUDBRIGHT
The National Trust for Scotland
Opening months and hours, check before visiting

Do not go to Kirkcudbright without calling in at Broughton House,

which was home and studio to the artist E.A. Hornel from 1901 until his death in 1933. The house and the furniture are ravishing and the gallery, designed by John Keppie, the associate of Charles Rennie Mackintosh, is very fine. I cannot imagine anyone not being bowled over by the garden and particularly this tree, as appropriately chosen and located as you could wish.

Hornel, like many of his contemporaries, had a keen interest in Japanese art, confirmed by a visit in 1893, aged 29. From his mid-30s onwards, he sold his paintings into a ready market. It gave him the wherewithal to buy this satisfying property in his family hometown, plus umpteen other houses in the High Street, to travel, to acquire 15,000 books and to develop the garden. It runs from the back of the house to a view over the river, full of incidents, surprises, deceptions, illusions and

secrets. Narrow paths between hedges lead you into and out of green rooms. Everything has been chosen with an eye for detail and quality. Children love it – what better test? There is much subtle use of stone for flags, troughs, steps, rockeries, sundials and the like. The structure and the stonework date from Hornel's time, as do some of the fruit trees, the sprawling, espaliered wisteria and the wall of climbing hydrangea. Most of the present plants were chosen by Davie Russel, gardener at Broughton House for a dozen years for the Hornel Trust and, since 1994, the NTS.

The Japanese influence is also evident in the first section of the garden, where this tree is an inspired choice, occupying centre stage of the view from the bow-window. Table dogwood grows in tiers anyway but the effect has been quietly emphasised by removing some intermediate branches. The foliage in this variety is particularly light and airy. Table dogwood was introduced from Japan before 1880. I have seen specimens occasionally in south Scotland – an excellent small tree, for example at Temple, Midlothian, another at Tyninghame, East Lothian. This variegated form, introduced by Veitch before 1890, is uncommon and a delight.

A recent report says that the dogwood is under a little stress, so Heather Insh has drawn, as a precaution, the very unstressed wisteria.

80. CABBAGE PALM *CORDYLINE AUSTRALIS*
BALCASKIE, BY PITTENWEEM
Sir Ralph Anstruther of that Ilk Bt
Open once a year in June under the Scotland's Gardens Scheme

Isn't it always a surprise to encounter a palm tree in Scotland, even if it isn't a true palm? They seem too exotic, too unpuritanical. You will meet these cabbage palms in most of the long-standing gardens up the west coast such as Logan, Brodick, Achamore on Gigha or Inverewe, and at Ullapool or Scourie. But they are a double surprise here by the coast of Fife, on the middle terrace at Balcaskie, in happy association with seventeenth-century walls, mown grass, rose beds, raked gravel, pedestalled urns, statues of gods or emperors and a house owned by the same family since 1698.

Cordyline (the e should be pronounced ee) is a member of the lily family – another surprise perhaps. The name comes from the Greek for a club because the fleshy roots of some species are club-like. It was brought to Britain from its native New Zealand in 1823. However unlikely, it has proved thoroughly at home in mild or sheltered coastal sites around Britain, often throwing root suckers and regenerating from seed. The tallest, at 50 ft, are in the Scillies; 30–40 ft is more usual but the east coast Balcaskie trees are noticeably smaller though they flower prodigiously and seem happy enough. They certainly coppice vigorously if cut deliberately or by cold winds.

They are important trees for the Maoris. The young shoots and the fleshy roots are eaten, while the leaves are used to make baskets and plaited into ropes.

There are many other excellent reasons for going to Balcaskie, not least that the house was built for his own occupation (1665–85) by a fine architect, Sir William Bruce. The classical avenues centre on the Bass Rock to the south-west and Kellie Law to the north-west and the beech hedges, following the curves and the dips or rises of the western approach, are as mesmerising as their designer, William Gilpin, intended.

Balcaskie, on a fine June afternoon, is one of the best places to be that I know – cabbage palms and all.

81. WINTER'S BARK *DRIMYS WINTERI*
LOGAN BOTANIC GARDEN, WIGTOWNSHIRE
Part of the Royal Botanic Garden Edinburgh
Opening hours

Given that Logan is renowned in tree circles for cabbage and Chusan palms, for eucalypts, southern beeches and eucryphias, it may seem a little perverse to single out this South American relation of the magnolias. I do so because we have few evergreens with big, loose, swags of seven-petalled, ivory flowers smelling delicately of jasmine. In any case it is not of much consequence what takes you to Logan, so long as you go.

Since 1969 Logan has been one of the constituent gardens of the RBGE. Considerations of scientific research and conservation came into play from that date and, clearly and properly, are central to policy today. All credit to the RBGE that they have also been faithful to the themes of the garden developed by the brothers Kenneth and Douglas McDouall in the long years between 1869 and 1945. It has been helpful that there have been only two curators since Logan became national property: Martin Colledge and Barry Unwin. For example, the famous avenue of 60 cabbage palms that the McDoualls planted across the Upper Walled Garden, most of which was then in very poor condition, was replaced in 1979.

What makes Logan different is the plant material. More of it is drawn from south of the equator than anywhere in Britain except perhaps at Tresco Abbey in the Scillies. The emphasis is on collections from the wild. All this is possible because of the benign climate of the Mull of Galloway, where such deep shelter has been established as to afford sufficient protection to the inner garden from the all-too-frequent, ferocious, salt-laden winds.

Winter's bark takes some hammering on its native patch since it grows in Tierra del Fuego and in southern Chile. The leaves on the tree at Logan are longish, oval and glossy, with smooth edges and rounded tips. Crushed, they smell mildly spicy. It was the bark though that was collected by Captain William Winter, sailing through the Strait of Magellan under Sir Francis Drake on the voyage of 1577–80. He used it to protect the crew against scurvy. Hence winter's bark.

82. CIDER GUM *EUCALYPTUS GUNNII* 'WHITTINGEHAMENSIS' WHITTINGEHAME TOWER, EAST LOTHIAN

The Earl of Balfour
Private but permission to visit readily granted
(See second photo section)

I suspect that somewhere there may be a detailed account of the Whittingehame gum and its offspring and this note may require revision. Can anyone help?

Bean says:

> Many of the trees in this country descend from the famous tree [blown down in the late 1960s] that grew at Whittingehame in East Lothian, a few miles from the North Sea. It was probably planted in 1853 and measured 96 x 19 ft in 1957. Its seed and seedlings were widely distributed and seem to have proved uniformly hardy. It has been suggested that it was a hybrid with *Eucalyptus urnigera*, but Maiden – in his day the foremost authority on the genus – considered it to be typical *E. gunnii.*

The tree is recorded in Elwes and Henry. They say that the seed was brought back from Tasmania by the Marquess of Salisbury, that the tree ripened seed most years about September, that the gardener collected and grew the seed and, most intriguingly, that 'the bark can be heard cracking in dry weather'.

A tree measured at Whittingehame in 1987 as 11 ft 8 in. is still listed as having the largest girth in Britain for this variety. The largest *E. gunnii* is listed as 16 ft 2 in. at Sidbury Manor in Dorset measured in 1990. All this is a bit doubtful given the growth rates of eucalypts and the near impossibility of exact identification. It does suggest, though, that all extant trees are well short of the original.

I measured one of the trees at the tower in 1996 as 12 ft 8 in. At that time it was not possible to measure the tree up beyond the house because long billets of wood were stacked against it. I think these may now have been removed. I have assumed that all the trees at Whittingehame are descendants from the original but I have no proof.

It would be interesting to try collecting and germinating seed. Doing so is usually straightforward, once you have permission. Perhaps the best source for eucalypts at the moment is Celyn Vale Nursery at the evocative address of Allt-y-Celyn, Carrog, Corwen, Clwyd.

83. EUCALYPTUS SPECIES
HIGH TREES, RAMSAY WOOD, GATEHOUSE OF FLEET
Drs R.G. and Barbara Law
Open by appointment

The Laws bought their property on the outskirts of Gatehouse of Fleet 20 years ago and moved in, on retirement, two years later. They have never been happier.

The house was built in an oakwood with a ground flora dominated by bracken. Dr Law wanted to grow trees which would reach a respectable size during his lifetime, remind him of early days in southern France (the rest of us may more readily think of umbrella pines and Italian cypresses, but there is no arguing with memories) and establish a connection with Tasmania, where a son now lives. The answer was eucalypts. Now he has over a hundred specimens of 52 species and, under agreement with the National Council for the Conservation of Plants and Gardens, holds one of the two National Collections of eucalypts.

By the standards of the eucalypts growing at Logan or Crarae or Kinlochhourn, High Trees is massively over-planted. But that is not the point. The purpose, aside from giving Dr Law much pleasure and exercise, is to be able to see, at close quarters, numerous different species of this puzzling genus. As he will tell you, he is not a gardener but a collector.

Among the eucalypts are numerous other Australasian trees, particularly species of *Nothofagus* and *Athrotaxis*, to say nothing of a very odd conifer called the celery topped pine or *Phyllocladus asplenifolius*. Most of the original oaks are still there, providing valuable if not absolute shelter from wind and frost. The bracken has all gone, every frond and rhizome hand-pulled by the Laws. What, in Dr Law's view, is the most hardy eucalypt for our conditions? – *E. pauciflora subsp. niphophila*. What is his favourite? – the *E. gunnii* that he planted first.

84. BEECH *FAGUS SYLVATICA*
NEWBATTLE ABBEY, DALKEITH
Newbattle Abbey College
Private but visitors welcome if they ask

Newbattle has been famous for beech trees for well over four centuries. Since beech is relatively short-lived, 200–250 years is the norm, this demonstrates foresight on the part of each generation. The most usual *coup de grâce* is wind, beech having a shallow root in relation to the vast sail area. It is likely that the first beech planted at Newbattle was amongst the first in Scotland of this English tree.

On 6 July 1789, Professor Walker measured a beech at what was then called Newbottle Abbey. 'Its trunk, where thickest, was seventeen feet in girth, and the span of the branches was eight-nine feet.' He thought it must have been planted between 1540 and 1560. The only others that he knew of about that age were at Ormiston Hall and at Oxenfoord Castle, both nearby, and at Taymouth. Sir Thomas Dick Lauder, to whom we owe this information, writes that the Newbattle tree was 'blown down a short time before 1809'.

At the beginning of last century the fattest, as distinct from tallest, beech in Britain was at Newbattle, 100 ft high, 21 ft girth, with an overall spread of 130 ft. The main stem of this tree blew down in about 1952, but seven separate new trunks from seven layered branches were already well established before it blew. They are now manifest trees, behind the big hedge at the back of the house. The largest is already 11 ft in girth and the whole is well on the way to becoming one of the most extraordinary arboricultural sights in the country.

While at Newbattle do not miss the beech on the front lawn: a near perfect tree, 100 ft high, 19 ft round and with space to breathe. If possible see it when the leaves are freshly open and the sun is behind them.

85. THE BEECH HEDGE *FAGUS SYLVATICA*
MEIKLEOUR, PERTHSHIRE
The Meikleour Trust
Beside the A93

In 1952 the notice board beside the Meikleour hedge read, 'This remarkable beech hedge, believed to have been planted about the year 1746, has been justly described as one of the arboreal wonders of the world. It is 580 yards long and has an average height of 85 feet.' The most recent measurements give the average height as 100 ft, reaching almost 120 ft at the northern end and 80 ft at the southern. These are natural heights. The hedge has not been topped. The height differential is masked because the road also rises south to north. Since 1966 the Meikleour hedge has appeared in the *Guinness Book of Records* as the highest in the world. I don't know the other contenders.

The hedge was planted by Jean Mercer of Meikleour and her husband Robert Murray Nairne. He was killed at Culloden. One version of folklore says that the hedge was allowed to grow as his memorial.

The lowest 15 ft is trimmed regularly in the interests of traffic safety. The upper part is now cut on a ten-year cycle mainly using loppers from a hydraulic platform. It takes four men up to six weeks. Charlie Fleming, who has done the work three times, says that enthusiasm sags before the end. All credit to the estate for digging into its pocket to keep this national treasure in such good shape, with modest help from the public purse.

Who can say how much life the hedge has yet? It is 250 years old, which is the normal maximum age for beech in Scotland. Trimming, like pollarding, reduces the area that has to be serviced by the roots and normally prolongs life. Conversely there are signs that the hedge is not in such good health as formerly, for which road salt and traffic fumes may bear some responsibility.

There is no mention of beech for hedging or anything else in John Reid's book of 1683, the first gardening manual in Scotland. Perhaps Jean Mercer had been reading the influential 1733 *Gardeners Dictionary* by Philip Miller of Chelsea. 'The Tree,' he says, 'is very proper to surround Plantations or large wilderness Quarters.' He adds, 'The Shade . . . is generally believed to be very salubrious to human Bodies.'

Perhaps this is also the oldest beech hedge in Scotland?

86. COMMON WALNUT *JUGLANS REGIA*
STIRLING CASTLE
Historic Scotland
Opening hours
(See second photo section)

Walnut has been planted over such a wide area and so long a timescale that it is impossible to discern the exact geographic origin. Whether this was the Near, Middle or Far East is immaterial since all are a great deal warmer than Scotland. It is therefore surprising and heartening to find this distinguished tree growing contentedly in virtually all quarters of this country. Alan Bremner and Elaine Bullard do not list it in their comprehensive *Trees and Shrubs in Orkney*. I assume it is not in Shetland either. I do not know about Caithness but there are some, for example, at Skibo Castle, Sutherland, in the Stornoway Castle woods and on Skye. John Miller lists many in his area particularly around the inner Moray and Cromarty Firths.

What walnut must have is a sufficient depth of soil to accommodate the deep, wide, root run and a respectable fertility. I could find nobody who could tell me the depth of the soil under the small lawn in the centre of Stirling Castle but there is a handsome, healthy, wide-spreading walnut, so it is clearly enough.

We look out from our Edinburgh home on to an 1870 walnut so are more than usually conscious of its virtues of bark, sinuous branches, summer mass and winter silhouette. It is very late into leaf and does not do much in the autumn, but, like all walnuts, it has a continuous air of quality. Conversely, it is a mildly irritating species under which to garden: there is scarcely a month of the year when twigs or budscales or aborted fruit or leaves or more twigs are not falling off the tree. Most are resistant to decay.

Walnuts are comparatively short-lived – 200 years is about the normal life expectancy. Since many of our present trees are of Victorian origin, the biggest of them about 10–12 ft girth, now is the time to be thinking about replacements.

Another surprise is that nuts, most puny and inedible by the standards of France, do germinate very occasionally in Scotland. I have found seedlings under the tree at Dr Gray's Hospital in Elgin and in a walled garden in Edinburgh.

87. PRICKLY CASTOR-OIL TREE *KALOPANAX PICTUS* VAR *MAXIMOWICZII*
DURRIS, BY BANCHORY
Mr J.W. Laing, West Lodge, Durris
Beside a private road but much used by all the public services

It is a close call whether the English or the Latin name is more of a turn-off from this singular tree. It is the only species in its genus, which is singular in an exact sense. It is also singular in the general sense; you will never mistake it for anything else. From a distance the form is clear. 'Gaunt' always seems a bit unkind so let us say 'very sparsely branched' or 'sculptural'. The bark is deeply furrowed. On a youngish tree there are clusters of vicious prickles. From close or far the foliage is, to quote

Bean, '. . . one of the most remarkable for cool temperate trees being very sparsely represented in the open air, though common enough in greenhouses'. Each leaf hangs on a longish hairy petiole and is palmate, five- to seven-lobed, with each lobe cut two-thirds to the base. To add to the exotic appearance, short shoots of leaves often grow directly from the trunk. *Kalopanax* is close to the family of the *Umbelliferae*, which is why the arrangement of the flowers and fruit may remind you of fennel or cow parsley.

The first *Kalopanax* that I ever saw was this tree on the drive into Durris House, in the company of enormous conifers. Some 25 years later the tree is still there, almost 8 ft in girth and as healthy as could be, albeit somewhat hemmed in by variegated holly and *Rhododendron ponticum*. The conifers are even more enormous.

There are two good trees at Dawyck and another pair at Stobo a few miles closer to Peebles. John Miller lists fine specimens at Dundonnell and Inverewe, which I have not seen, and at Leckmelm near Ullapool, which I have. This last is inside an iron guard, presumably to protect the passer-by from the prickles. The leaves of the *Kalopanax* are variable across its huge range, which includes Japan, Korea, China and eastern Russia. The tree in the RBGE is the type with much larger leaves. It is labelled *K. septemlobum*, an older name.

'Chinese,' Wilson writes '. . . for making the drums used on boats and in temples the wood of this tree, Tzu-ch'in shu [the Chinese name for the prickly castor-oil tree], is considered best, being easily worked, pliable and resonant'. Alan Coombes says that the leaves are edible when young.

88. BLACK MULBERRY *MORUS NIGRA*
LUFFNESS, ABERLADY, EAST LOTHIAN
Luffness Limited
Open under the Scotland's Gardens Scheme
(See second photo section)

The mulberry that I knew first in Scotland stands in the Cooper Park, Elgin. When we lived in the town the mulberry was surrounded by a cage for canaries and ornamental fowl, which made the ripe fruit frustratingly difficult to get at. Those that you could reach were as delicious as any mulberries anywhere. To my mind this is the prince of fruit. It is not better known, perhaps, because it will not pack or travel and because everything – fingers, mouths, clothes, grandchildren – becomes purple-stained at the least encounter.

The mulberry at Luffness is taller than the Elgin tree, 25 ft, and it has a fatter trunk, 4 ft round. It hangs over the path just inside the garden gate, the large, wrinkly leaves more or less brushing your nose. I am told that it fruits prodigiously.

Contrary to almost universal belief, mulberries grow at a respectable rate. I know a youngster in south Edinburgh which is putting on an annual growth of 18 in. or more. There is a vigorous tree planted by the Queen Mother during 1976 in the imaginative garden of Haddington House. The Luffness tree might not be older than 80 years, however venerable it may look.

The black mulberry has been cultivated for so long that its natural origins are obscure – perhaps Iran. There are three other things to know about this classical tree. The leaves do not unfold until almost all risk of frost is past. Mulberries are easy to propagate from 'truncheons' or lengths of wood about as thick as a truncheon, taken off mature trees. Finally, unlike almost every other tree, no one anywhere, ever, has found a single variant.

89. SOUTHERN BEECHES *NOTHOFAGUS SPP.*
CRARAE, BY INVERARY, ARGYLL
The Crarae Gardens Charitable Trust
Opening hours

I went first to Crarae in October 1978. It was my first experience of the use on this grand scale of innumerable introduced trees for, simultaneously, their intrinsic beauty and as shelter for the innumerable shrubs below. It is not an arboretum like Scone. It is not, except on the flat, a garden with scattered trees. It is not, like Kilmun, a collection primarily for scientific purpose, though that comes into it on the top of the hill. Crarae is, or most of its 16 ha are, a dense, complex woodland garden. It is a source of fascination and delight for everyone on any day of the year but reaches an exuberant climax in October.

It is quite a thought that virtually every tree and shrub has been planted here by three generations of Campbells or the Trust, with serious thought given to how each would fit in to the increasingly complex appearance of the whole. Lady Campbell of Succoth started Crarae in 1912. Her son Sir George Campbell hugely increased the area and the collection until his death in 1967, as did his son Sir Islay Campbell until he made the garden over to a Charitable Trust in 1978. No doubt there have been failures and partial failures along the way, but contemplate the depth of knowledge needed to get so much right. It is difficult to change your mind about a tree after the first decade or two. A ruthless judgement has always had to be an attribute of the best gardeners.

The Trust is struggling to make ends meet and has invited the NTS to take over, on the grounds that in order to survive Crarae now needs their scale, professionalism and marketing skills. It is, I hope, inconceivable that a solution will not be found.

From the wealth of trees here, I want to focus on the southern beeches, an enjoyable, and rewarding, genus. You will find not uncommonly across Scotland, three southern beeches, all deciduous. With a good deal of hunting about, particularly in the west, you will

find a further eight, one deciduous, the rest evergreen. Much simpler is
to spend some hours at Crarae, where they all grow and grow
particularly well.

Sir George started planting southern beeches in the 1930s and
increased their number after a visit to Chile in 1952. (Six are South
Americans, four New Zealanders and one Tasmanian.) All the
evergreens have copious, small, dark-green leaves, elegantly arranged. If
I had to choose one, it would be the silver beech from New Zealand that
has bark like a cherry. In Latin, it is named for Archibald Menzies,
Nothofagus menziesii. There is one in the RBGE, in a particularly
sheltered corner.

A pleasant feature of many older west coast southern beeches is that
they are surrounded by carpets of naturally regenerated seedlings. Many
are hybrids between parents that may not grow within hundreds of miles
of each other in the wild, perhaps not even on the same continent. You
can see examples of this regeneration at Benmore Botanic Garden,
Inverewe and perhaps most densely at Crarae itself.

90. ORIENTAL PLANE *PLATANUS ORIENTALIS*
TYNINGHAME WALLED GARDEN, EAST LOTHIAN
Mr and Mrs C.A.H. Gwyn
Open under Scotland's Garden Scheme
(See second photo section)

I would rate the half-hectare of trees within the walled garden at
Tyninghame in the class of Crathes, Keir, Cluny House, Brechin Castle,
Falkland Palace, Crarae or Glendoick. They have been excellently
chosen not only for their aesthetics but in many cases for being at, but
not past, the limit of willingness to grow healthily in Scotland. The
species here tend to be spoken about in botanical Latin because their
English names often sound odd or invented. Japanese varnish tree will
not ring many bells whereas, if you are interested in specimen trees at
all, *Rhus potaninii*, which is here, will get you into a reasonably well-

known genus and may remind you that Grigori Nikolaevich Potanin (1835–1920) was a prodigiously successful explorer of central and eastern Asia, also with a larch to his name. In English or in Latin, the oriental plane at Tyninghame is an inspired choice.

If you know an oriental plane from further south you would not plant one in a confined space. The tree at Chilton Foliat, Wiltshire, is nearly 30 ft round. If you know an oriental plane from the eastern Mediterranean, Iran, Afghanistan or Kashmir, you would hesitate before planting one unless you had half a football pitch to spare. Xerxes halted his army for three days to give his troops and himself adequate opportunity to admire the first oriental plane he had seen. These considerations do not arise in Scotland. The largest it is likely to reach is along the lines of a tree in the RBGE.

This tree has been placed alongside a western plane or buttonwood from North America to make the point that these are the parents of a hybrid – London plane – which, for 150 years or more, has been the principal urban tree not only of London but of Paris and umpteen towns and cities elsewhere.

The leaves of the oriental plane are deeply enjoyable. They are five-fingered, cut almost to the base and bright green. They make elegant stars on their own and a delicate filigree in their mass. According to one granddaughter, they also make the best fallen leaves for kicking up, for rolling in and for having leaf fights. As is customary with grandfathers, I would not dream of contradicting her.

91. EUGENE'S POPLAR *POPULUS X CANADENSIS* 'EUGENI'
ROYAL BOTANIC GARDEN EDINBURGH
Royal Botanic Garden
Opening hours
(See second photo section)

After every major gale I hasten down to the RBGE, like a mother hen, to see how the trees have fared and particularly whether the two majestic Eugene's poplars are still standing. There I will find Derek Beavis, who is responsible for trees in the garden, assessing the damage, organising his tree surgeons and planning replacements. He tells me that one of the poplars will have to be taken down, rot having been discovered in the trunk. He is not averse to change. He needs space for new trees. The thrust these days, very properly, is towards trees from wild-collected seed of conservation interest, particularly where the natural populations are rare or threatened.

The taller of the poplars is 120 ft, which makes it easily the tallest tree in Edinburgh and amongst the tallest broadleaves in Scotland. Probably the only taller trees are a beech and an ash in the Carse of Gowrie. About equal are a sessile oak near Conon Bridge and a large-leaved lime at Scone Palace. Not far behind are an elm, also in the Carse, and the Duke of Buccleuch's sycamore at Drumlanrig.

Eugene's poplar was found in 1832, a chance hybrid seedling in the nursery founded by Gabriel Simon at Metz in France. He named it, charmingly, after his three-year-old son, Eugene. The original Metz tree grew at a phenomenal rate reaching 150 ft and 20 ft in girth by 1900. Cuttings were introduced to Kew, to Glasnevin in Dublin and to Edinburgh in 1888. So, in Edinburgh, you are looking at 120 ft in 112 years.

The RBGE is not, of course, so concerned about growth statistics but about research, conservation and education, at the leading edge of what will be needed in the twenty-first century. As everybody knows, these serious, not to say, crucial tasks are fully compatible with maintaining a wonderful green pleasance in the heart of Edinburgh.

I have known the garden on and off for over four decades. There are something like a couple of hundred favourite trees to keep an eye on during spring, summer, autumn and winter. Among them are two other poplars. The first, on the path from the Inverleith gate to the glasshouses, was discovered and introduced by, and named after, 'Chinese' Wilson. The pleasant feature of *Populus wilsonii* is that the leaves rattle – no other word will do. The second poplar, up the path opposite the Chinese garden, is *Populus maximowiczii*, a native of Japan, Manchuria, Korea and eastern Russia. It is as handsome and distinctive as you could wish. It is named for Carl Ivanovich Maximowicz, pronounced 'Maksimovich' (1827–91), an energetic and distinguished Russian botanist. It is curious that this is one of the very few in Scotland given that it is, in my experience, as easy to propagate as most poplars.

92. CHINESE NECKLACE POPLAR *POPULUS LASIOCARPA*
BRODICK CASTLE, ISLE OF ARRAN
The National Trust for Scotland
Opening hours
(See second photo section)

Within a confusing genus, only the very rare *Populus wilsonii* has leaves approaching in size those of the Chinese necklace poplar. Not only are they big – 20 cm long by 15 cm wide is the mean – but they are pleasantly distinctive with a heart-shaped base, a drawn out, slightly twisted tip, set round with little teeth and the main veins, midribs and stalk are a rhubarb red.

I remember meeting this poplar at The Hirsel, Coldstream, at Carberry Tower, near Musselburgh, at Dawyck, at Brechin Castle and elsewhere, but my first encounter was with the specimen in the complex garden at Brodick in the company of the then head gardener, John Bashford. It was he who told me that *Populus lasiocarpa* was unusual, perhaps unique amongst poplars, because the catkins are polygamous, meaning that male and female flowers are on the same stalk. *Lasiocarpa* means 'woolly seeded', and so they are. The trunks are long and scaly; the branches tend to be few, longish and level. The presence of a Chinese necklace poplar is usually an indicator that there will be more quality trees around, as at Brodick.

This is one of the trees introduced by 'Chinese' Wilson. He is quoted in Bean as saying:

> Mr Wilson told me that on one of his journeys he came to a little Chinese farm where a farmer had made an enclosure for his animals by driving stakes in the ground. These were *P. lasiocarpa* and they had taken root and grown freely.

The story is the more interesting because, here in Scotland, this species, unlike most poplars, is difficult to strike from cuttings, or so I read.

93. TIBETAN CHERRY *PRUNUS SERRULA*
CLUNY HOUSE GARDEN, ABERFELDY
Wendy and John Mattingley
Opening hours
(See second photo section)

The garden at Cluny House is the creation, since 1950, of Mr Masterton, in the intervals of being the local vet, and of his wife. It has been maintained and developed by their daughter and son-in-law, the Mattingleys. It is a satisfying and encouraging demonstration of what can be done in half a century, albeit, before the Mastertons, there were a few conifers planted in the period 1850–80. These included the now massive giant sequoia, which, at 35 ft in girth, many dendrologists reckon to be the largest in Britain.

A preoccupation of the Mastertons was to grow plants introduced by Ludlow and Sheriff after their Himalayan expeditions in the 1930s, particularly primulas, poppies and lilies. As Cluny House sits on a shelf above the Tay between Weem and Strathtay, the moist cool summers and dry winters there are ideal for these chosen plants. But there also had to be protection from cold winds. Shelter was established by mass tree planting down the steepish bank below the house. Narrow paths zigzag down the slope, linking small glades below the canopy. The trees are a wonderfully motley collection of what will grow – pines, spruces, silver firs, cypresses, birches, rowans and southern beeches.

Until recently the tree to head for was the Manchurian cherry, *Prunus maackii*, after the Russian naturalist Richard Maack. Bean is, unusually, a bit sniffy about Manchurian cherry. 'It has,' he says, 'a very distinctive yellowish brown, lustrous bark, but has no other claim to a place in gardens.' He might have said that the bark is a bright shining brown, shading from honey to orange and that the flowers are deliciously scented. The racemes are like our native bird cherry but gowing on last year's wood. Alas, the Cluny tree has had to be taken down, having lost a big limb in a gale. I imagine that the Mattingleys will want another.

Turn your attention meanwhile, to the Tibetan cherry. This is one of the most desirable trees to arrive last century. The bark on a young tree is glossy, smooth and red-brown. Older trees, like this one at Cluny, begin to lose their gloss but replace it with a splendid shagginess, approaching the coat of a Shetland pony. The Cluny tree is from seed collected by Ludlow and Sheriff and given to Wendy's father in 1948. In her words, 'it produces thousands of cherries virtually every year and these are regenerating throughout the garden'.

Plant Tibetan cherry outside a north-facing window, where the sun will strike the bark in your view, an old trick perhaps in danger of being forgotten?

94. HUNGARIAN OAK *QUERCUS FRAINETTO*
CARBERRY TOWER, BY MUSSELBURGH
The Church of Scotland
Private but visitors welcome if they ask

Some of the best Hungarian oaks in Britain grow around Edinburgh, Perth and Dundee, perhaps because they were introduced around 1835 by Charles Lawson, a nurseryman in Edinburgh. There are fine trees at Dalmeny, the RBGE, the Riccarton campus of Heriot-Watt University (on an odd-looking tump outside the principal entrance), Dawyck,

Kinfauns Hotel east of Perth and Camperdown Park, Dundee. For my money, the finest of them all and a very fine tree indeed is this one at Carberry.

It is perfectly placed five or six tree lengths from the house, an appropriate setting for a wide-spreading powerful statement of a tree, over 100 ft high and 15 ft round. The leaves are shaped like our native sessile oak but they are twice as big. They are widely spaced so that the whole crown appears like an intricately carved screen through which to see a fragmented sun, or, if you are fortunate, a rising, pale-silver moon. Autumn colour may be brief but it can be rich in yellows and reds of many hues. The principal winter pleasure of Hungarian oak is given by the long, strong branches radiating from a smooth round trunk.

The name Hungarian oak is delimiting since it grows naturally across the Balkans and in southern Italy as well as Hungary. It appears moreover that *frainetto* is a mistake for *farnetto*, the Italian name for the tree but the rules of botanical nomenclature do not allow mistakes to be corrected.

I do not have a date for the Carberry tree though it seems likely it was put there by the 15th Baron Elphinstone, who succeeded his father in 1861 and was an 'ardent horticulturalist'. The house, known as Carberry Tower, was gifted to the Church of Scotland in 1961. With your back to the Hungarian oak you can look across to Carberry Hill, where, on 15 June 1567, Mary Queen of Scots surrendered to the Scottish lords.

95. LUCOMBE OAK *QUERCUS X HISPANICA* 'LUCOMBEANA'
INNES HOUSE, NEAR ELGIN, MORAY
Mr and Mrs Mark Tennant
Open to parties by appointment
(See second photo section for another example)

The parents of the Lucombe oak are the Turkey oak, *Quercus cerris*, and the cork oak, *Quercus suber*. The first grows with panache in all of lowland Scotland from Skibo to Kelso. The second is a poor thing in the RBGE and more or less anywhere else in Britain outside Devon and Cornwall, though, to my surprise, there is a reasonable tree in the Chelsea Physic Garden in London. The hybrid occurs in the wild and has been cultivated on a number of occasions. The hybrids bear fertile acorns but, since these arise from back-crossing with the parents, they do not have the hybrid vigour of the first generation. All rather confusing perhaps, but the upshot is that there are various clones which vary between the vigour of *Q. cerris* and the evergreen corkiness of *Q. suber.*

This version of the hybrid was raised in, and massively distributed from, the Exeter nursery of William Lucombe in the middle of the eighteenth century. The fame of the tree preceded the distribution. The very fine tree at Innes was noted in a list of plants drawn up by A. Cooper Esquire, advocate to the Earl of Fife in 1794, as 'No 272 *Quercus Exoniensis,* Exeter evergreen oak'. It adds an extra pleasure when you know where a tree came from and when.

While at Innes, enjoy the wonderfully full-crowned, photogenic larch dating from about 1745 and the trees planted between 1929 and 1934 by the present owner's grandfather. He bought extensively from Hilliers, Marchant of Wimborne, Robert Veitch of Exeter, Gomer Waterer of Knaphill and White of Sunningdale. Many plants perished but many survived. Some, in growing well, have changed views about success and failure in the north-east. The birches are particularly well represented with *Betula lutea, B. papyrifera, B. maximowicziana* and *B. albosinensis var. septentrionalis.* But pride of place should go to the Japanese horse chestnut, the Chinese beech and the Madrona.

A Fulham oak, no longer there, had its leading shoot shot off by the butler, while he was 'potting rats from an upstairs window' – an unusual, perhaps unprecedented fate!

96. CHINESE EUODIA *TETRADIUM DANIEILLII*
GLENDOICK, PERTHSHIRE
Peter Cox
Open from time to time under the Scotland's Gardens Scheme

Around about 1943 Miss Carruthers, known behind her back as Nell the Bull, pointed to the Carse of Gowrie on the oilcloth wall map of Scotland in Class 1 of Jedburgh Grammar School, and said, 'This, children, is Paradise on Earth'. I believed her then and am inclined to believe her now.

As you go east from Perth there are, on the slopes to the north, a series of wondrous tree places – Branklyn, Kinfauns, Glendoick, Fingask and Ballindean. Their owners may complain that their summers are too dry but most of us would be well content with these growing conditions, especially if our predecessors had had the good sense to establish thick, tall, reliable shelter around the gardens proper.

Even in this company Glendoick is exceptional because the owner may say, modestly but accurately, 'this is from seed that I collected in China or Chile', or some place that most of the rest of us can only dream about. Peter Cox is the second in the plant-collecting dynasty 'founded' by his father E.H.M. Cox, who went off to Upper Burma with Reginald Farrer in 1919. He is now joined by his son Kenneth. Their speciality is rhododendrons but they are no slouches when it comes to trees. Indeed, one of the best books rehearsing knowledge about garden trees in Scotland is *Modern Trees* by E.H.M and P.A. Cox published in 1961. It is packed with first-hand knowledge.

Glendoick has splendid trees: the Indian chestnuts and their numerous seedlings, the Dahurian larch, the many southern beeches; the huge birch-leafed maple and the pair of western yellow pines, but the most interesting is this Chinaman.

Everything about it is pleasing except the name. Taxonomists have constantly changed their minds about what it should be called in Latin. There are too few around for anyone to have coined anything in decent

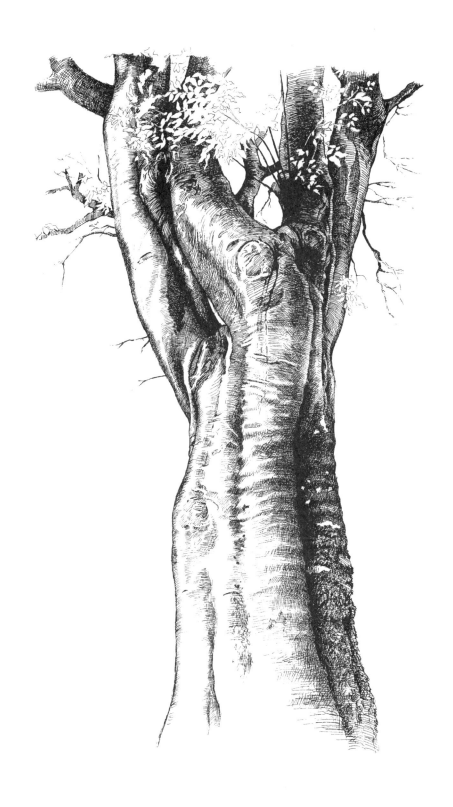

English. So it all too frequently goes unrecognised and unsung. At Glendoick it is a must-see, whether for the smooth, elephantine-wrinkled bark, the vast spread of branches, the elegant 'leafscape', the clusters of very late flowers, or the fruit – first orange, then red.

Tetradium daniellii was first discovered by a European, William Daniell, a surgeon with the British army, around 1860. The tree at Glendoick came from seed collected by 'Chinese' Wilson during his 1907–08 expedition into Hupeh and was planted here in 1923. It is now nearly 13 ft round – the biggest in Britain.

97. SMALL LEAVED LIME *TILIA CORDATA*
ARNISTON, GOREBRIDGE, MIDLOTHIAN
Mrs Althea Dundas Bekker
Opening hours
(See second photo section)

There are two European limes, the small leaved and the large leaved. Both are native in England, the former extensively, the latter very sparsely. Neither is native in Scotland. When planted, many grow particularly well. At an unknown date and place, these limes produced a hybrid, known as the common lime. The common lime is now ubiquitous though, to many eyes, more ungainly than either parent.

From the late seventeenth century, for at least 100 years, the common lime was the fashionable tree for planting avenues. You will see them at Traquair, Peebles-shire, for example, or Drummond Castle, Perthshire or at Longforgan, near Dundee or here at Arniston, Midlothian.

In flower or fruit, the common lime is readily separable from the large leaved because, although both hang below the shoot, the former has five or six flowers and then fruit in a cluster while the large leaved has three. In marked contrast, the flowers and fruit of the small leaved lime are above the shoot, bright yellow and attached to small green bracts. This arrangement means that the entire crown of a flowering tree is yellow. The leaves are smaller, rounder, pale blue on the underside and retained longer. For too long I thought that big burrs on a tree and a flurry of side shoots meant that it must be common lime. In fact these features can develop almost as strongly on the small leaved. The overall structure of this lime is, however, always simpler, clearer and more tree-like.

With all these features in mind it is instructive to look for small leaved lime in July. They are fairly uncommon, especially north of Dunkeld, but more common than is often supposed. In south Edinburgh they make up about 5 per cent of the extensive lime population. There are big trees on the North Inch in Perth, for example, at Scone, at the Auchterarder House Hotel or at Drumlanrig, Dumfriesshire. The huge isolated tree on the lawn outside Bush House, Roslin, is this species. Most satisfactorily presented, however, are three trees at Arniston, all probably remnants of the trees laid out in 1726 to the plan of William Adam for Robert Dundas, 2nd Lord Arniston. Two of the trees finish the avenue of common limes. The larger has a girth of 20 ft though, admittedly, only because of a vast side branch.

98. SILVER PENDENT LIME *TILIA X PETIOLARIS*
KILLIECHASSIE HOUSE, NEAR ABERFELDY
J.K. Rowling
Private but visible from the minor road between Weem and
  Edradynate

Who needs big trees these days, widely spaced, over grass – the traditional parkland scene? The answer is a surprisingly large number of people. It is by no means only country house owners renewing their surrounds but all organisations and authorities with breathing space around their buildings, be that high-tech industries, hospitals, science parks, universities, out-of-town shopping centres, prisons, residential homes or prestige headquarters. Big trees are the cheapest, most effective means of tying buildings into the landscape and, surprisingly quickly, creating a sense of permanence. The trees need to grow big while remaining healthy and bosky. Nothing exotic is required. Traditional

species will do very well – oaks, limes, sweet chestnut, horse chestnut, sycamore, beech – but a deeply satisfying addition to the suite is the silver pendent lime.

You will see it from time to time in big gardens. There is a stunning tree at Mortonhall House on the southern edge of Edinburgh for example, but if you want to see it in a contented parkland setting, pause on the minor road between Weem and Edradynate, and look up at this warm slope above the Tay. If you can see a 150 ft Sitka spruce at the top of the bank, you are in the right place. The tree you are looking for is nearly 100 ft tall and over 13 ft round, identifiable by the cascades of silver-backed leaves. The flowers are amongst the latest of the limes, blooming at the end of July, massed and very fragrant. Silver pendent lime has not been found in the wild. All trees are grafts usually on a broad-leaved lime.

There is some controversy about silver pendent lime and bees. I met Miles Hadfield, writer, botanist and gardener, on a number of occasions and, then and now, have a huge admiration for his acute observation and determination to check everything himself. This is what he had to say on the subject:

> In some seasons, but by no means every year, many bees appear to be overcome by some narcotic effect of the nectar. While stupefied they are often attacked and killed by various enemies, but the nectar itself does not seem to be poisonous. The effect is surprisingly variable, and may even be dependent on the individual tree or its situation.

Some authorities think that *Tilia x petiolaris* is a variant of the silver lime, *Tilia tomentosa*, but that does not really matter since the tree is so distinct.

99. *TROCHODENDRON ARALIOIDES*
ARDUAINE, KILMELFORD, ARGYLL
The National Trust for Scotland
Opening hours

The rain had been torrential all morning. I arrived at Arduaine, pronounced Ardoonie, just at that perfect moment when the heavens relent. The air was washed clean, the sun was warm and the bright sea cluttered with islands – Luing, Lunga, Scarba, Shuna, Jura, Mull in the distance. Admirable circumstances to enjoy one of the indisputably great gardens of Scotland.

What makes Arduaine, what makes any garden, great? There must be a passage of time. Try as you will, you cannot establish framework trees much under a century. Throughout that time or through most of it, you must have knowledge, commitment, hard work and cash. James Arthur Campbell turned the first sod at Arduaine in 1898 and saw the garden through the early establishment phase until his death in 1929. Three generations of Campbell descendants and their staff kept the garden going through the difficult mid-century years until it passed, in 1971, to the brothers Wright, originally nurserymen from Essex. It was gifted to the NTS in 1992. Maurice Wilkins is the head gardener. As you come down the hill past the sprawling hotel you are entering something that did not have to exist and only exists in its complex detail because it has received a century of dedication from at least a dozen people. It is an exciting thought and a humbling one.

The NTS 26-page, full-colour garden guide is excellent value at three pounds. There is also a list and description of 75 significant plants, equally excellent. The framework trees at Arduaine are dense on the ground as they have to be, well chosen and in good fettle. Among the special trees, I particularly enjoyed the numerous big magnolias, many eucryphias, a substantial Chinese hazel, a favourite big-leaved maple and a huge southern beech, the identity of which experts ponder over.

Pride of place must, however, go to this evergreen tree from Japan,

Formosa and Korea. It is insufficiently common to have acquired an English name – 'ivy tree' might suit – and goes by the sonorous Latin of *Trochodendron aralioides*. At 60 ft tall and 7 ft round it is the largest in Britain by a furlong. The leaves are bright apple-green, leathery, apparently unpalatable to any insect and held on stalks as long as the leaf blade. There are curious green flowers without sepals or petals but with a circle of stamens that give rise to the first part of the name; *Trochos* is Greek for a wheel. The bark is aromatic, an enjoyable attribute of any plant.

100. *ZELKOVA VERSCHAFFELTII*
CRATHES, BY BANCHORY
The National Trust for Scotland
Opening hours
(See second photo section)

If you meet a zelkova anywhere, you know that you are in knowledgeable arboricultural hands. If you meet Verschaffelt's zelkova, you know that you are in exceptional hands. It should be no surprise to find one at Crathes, prominent on the path up to the castle from the car park, since, to my mind, the trees at Crathes are just about as good as garden trees get.

The grey-mottled bark is pleasant but the leaves are why you should grow this smallish, bushy-topped tree. They are about two inches long, oval and with six to nine regular, triangular teeth like a diminutive bowsaw. The filigree effect, especially when seen against the sky, as at Crathes, is dazzling. Although the tree has been in cultivation at Kew since 1886, nobody knows its origin or appears to have seen one in the wild. From various routes, experts think it may be from the Caucasus. It is named for Ambrose Colletto Alexandre Verschaffelt (1825–86) of Ghent, nurseryman and author of a book on camellias.

The zelkovas are five tree species, closely allied to the elms, one from Crete, two from China and Japan and, if the hypothesis about

Vershaffelt is correct, two from the Caucasus. Zelkova, incidentally, is the Caucasian name for their common tree. I am particularly fond of *Zelkova carpinifolia* because it was just about the first exotic tree to which I paid close attention. That was in 1960. I had met Alan Mitchell at the Forestry Commission Research Station at Alice Holt in Surrey and he had asked me to check whether the tree at Pitt Farm, Chudleigh, over Haldon Hill south of Exeter, was still there. It was an extraordinary and unforgettable mass of upright stems, curling over at the top, more like a pollard than a tree. Since then I have seen very few. The most astonishing, a big tree, is tucked away on a farm in east Scotland, which prefers to remain anonymous.

There are three *Zelkova serratas* from the Far East in the RBGE, all particularly happy and particularly attractive. There is, or was, another in the Aberdeen University Botanic Garden and we planted several in the Winding Walks outside Fochabers in the 1970s. I do not know if any survived.

I was heartened to see that zelkovas had been planted recently in Kelvingrove, Glasgow. That is just the place for such large, interesting, elegant trees, preferably planted by the dozen.

BIBLIOGRAPHY

THE ESSENTIAL REFERENCES

Anderson, Mark. L. (1967), *The History of Scottish Forestry*, Thomas Nelson, London

Bean, W.J. (1914, 8th Edition revised 1970), *Trees and Shrubs Hardy in the British Isles*, John Murray, London

Elwes, H.J. and Henry, A.H. (1906–13), *The Trees of Great Britain and Ireland*, privately printed, 7 vols., Edinburgh

Hadfield, Miles (1957), *British Trees*, J.M. Dent, London

Hamilton, Thomas (6th Earl of Haddington), ed. Professor M.L. Anderson (1953), *Some Directions about raising Forest Trees*, Thomas Nelson, London

Leathart, Scott (1991), *Whence Our Trees*, Foulsham, Slough

Mitchell, Alan (1972), *Conifers in the British Isles*, Forestry Commission Booklet 33, HMSO, London

Mitchell, Alan (1974), A *Field Guide to the Trees of Britain and Northern Europe*, HarperCollins, London

Mitchell, Alan (1996), *Alan Mitchell's Trees of Britain*, HarperCollins, London

Rackham, Oliver (1976, revised 1990), *Trees and Woodland in the British Landscape*, J.M. Dent, London

Smout, T.C. (ed.) (1997), *Scottish Woodland History*, Scottish Cultural Press, Edinburgh

Stearn, William. T. (1972, revised 1992), *Dictionary of Plant Names for Gardeners*, Cassell, London

Steven, H.M. and Carlisle, A. (1959), *The Native Pinewoods of Scotland*, Oliver and Boyd, Edinburgh

OTHER REFERENCES

Anderson, Mark L. (1950), *The Selection of Tree Species*, Oliver and Boyd, Edinburgh

Banks, W. B. and Cooper, R.J. (1997), 'Utilization of Softwoods in Great Britain', *Forestry* 70

Boutcher, William (1775), *A Treatise on Forest-Trees*, R. Fleming, Edinburgh

Brasier, Clive (1996), 'New Horizons in Dutch Elm Disease Control', *Report on Forest Research, 1996*, Forestry Commission, Edinburgh

Bremner, Alan H. and Bullard, Elaine R. (undated), *Trees and Shrubs in Orkney*, private publication

Bunce, R.G.H. and Jeffers, J.N.R. (eds.) (1976), *Native Pinewoods of Scotland: Proceedings Aviemore Symposium 1975*, Institute of Terrestrial Ecology, Cambridge

Carmichael, Alexander (1992 edition), *Carmina Gadelica*, Floris Books, Edinburgh

Chambers, F.M. (ed.) (1993), *Climatic Change and Human Impact on the Landscape*, Chapman and Hall, London

Clapham, A.R., Tutin, T.G. and Warburg, E.F. (1952), *Flora of the British Isles*, Cambridge University Press, Cambridge

Colvin, Brenda (1947), *Trees for Town and Country*, John Murray, London

Cook, Moses (1717), *The Manner of Raising, Ordering and Improving Forest-Trees*, printed for Daniel Browne, Andrew Bell (and others), London

Cox, E.H.M. and Cox, P.A. (1961), *Modern Trees*, Thomas Nelson, London

Darling, F.F. (1955), *West Highland Survey*, Oxford University Press, Oxford

Darwin, Tess (1996), *The Scots Herbal*, Mercat Press, Edinburgh

Dickson, J.H. (1993), 'The Yew Tree (Taxus baccata L.) in Scotland – Native or Early Introduction or Both?', *Scottish Forestry* 48

Donaldson, James (1794), *General View of the Agriculture of the County of Elgin or Moray*, Board of Agriculture

Dougall, Martin and Dickson, Jim (1997), 'Old Managed Oaks in the Glasgow Area', in T.C. Smout, (ed.) (1997), *Scottish Woodland History*, Scottish Cultural Press, Edinburgh

Edwards, Ian (1999), 'The Tree Planters' Guide to Sitka Spruce', *Reforesting Scotland* 21

Evelyn, John (1664), *Sylva, or a Discourse of Forest-Trees*, John Martyn and James Allestry, Printers to the Royal Society, London

Fairbairn, W.A. (1972), 'Dalkeith Old Wood', *Scottish Forestry* 26

Fairbrother, Nan (1970), *New Lives, New Landscapes*, The Architectural Press, London

Forestry Commission (1998), *Caledonian Pinewood Inventory*, Forestry Commission, Edinburgh

Gilbert-Carter, H. (1936), *British Trees and Shrubs*, Oxford University Press, Oxford

Gilbert-Carter, H. (1950), *Glossary of the British Flora*, Cambridge University Press, Cambridge

Gilpin, William (ed. Lauder, Sir Thomas Dick) (1834), *Remarks on Forest Scenery*, Fraser & Co. Edinburgh, Smith, Elder & Co., London

Grigson, Geoffrey (1958), *The Englishman's Flora*, Phoenix House, London

Hunter, Thomas (1883), *Woods, Forests and Estates of Perthshire*, Henderson, Robertson and Hunter, Perth

Hutchison, Robert, of Carlowrie (1874–75), 'Old and Remarkable Trees in Britain', in the *Transactions of the Scottish Arboricultural Society*, vol. VII, Neill & Co., Edinburgh

Langton, Chris (1995), 'New Pinewoods on the Atholl Estate', in J.R. Aldhous (ed.), *Our Pinewood Heritage*, Proc. Conf. at Inverness, Bell & Blain, Glasgow

Lauder, Sir Thomas Dick (1830 edition of 1998), *The Great Moray Floods of 1829*, Moray Books, Forres

Laughton Johnston, J. (2000), *Scotland's Nature in Trust*, The National Trust for Scotland, T. & A.D. Poyser, London

Loudon, John Claudius (1838), *Arboretum et Fruticetum Britannicum*, Longman, Orme, Brown, Green and Longmans, London

Lusby, Philip and Wright, Jenny (1996), *Scottish Wild Plants*, The Stationery Office Ltd, Edinburgh for the Royal Botanic Garden Edinburgh

Mabey, Richard (1996), *Flora Britannica*, Sinclair-Stevenson, London

Mackay, Donald (1995), *Scotland's Rural Land Use Agencies*, Scottish Cultural Press, Aberdeen

MacKenzie, Neil A. (1999), 'The Native Woodland Resource of Scotland', *Forestry Commission Technical Paper* 30, Forestry Commission, Edinburgh

Mackenzie, Osgood (1921, edition of 1994), *A Hundred Years in the Highlands*, Birlinn Ltd, Edinburgh

McCallum Webster, Mary (1978), *Flora of Moray, Nairn and East Inverness*, Abcrdeen University Press, Aberdeen

McVean, D.N. and Ratcliffe, D.A. (1962), *Plant Communities of the Scottish Highlands*, Monographs Nature Conservancy, London

Meredith, Allan, quoted in J. Edward Milner (1992), *The Tree Book*, Collins & Brown, London

Miller, John (1999), *Trees of the Northern Highlands*, John Miller, Alness

Miller, Philip (1733), *The Gardeners Dictionary* , printed for the author, London

Mitchell, Alan F., Schilling, Victoria E. and White, John E.J. (1995), 'Champion Trees in the British Isles', *Technical Paper* 7, Forestry Commission, Edinburgh

Mitchell, Ann Lindsay and House, Syd (1999), *David Douglas*, Autumn Press, London

Newton, A. C. and Ashmole, P. (1998), *Native Woodland Restoration in Southern Scotland*, Report of a discussion meeting held at the RBGE in November 1997, The Borders Forest Trust, Jedburgh

Nixon, Chris and Cameron, Ewan (1994), 'A Pilot Study of the Age,

Structure and Viability of the Mar Lodge Pinewoods', *Scottish Forestry* 48

Pakenham, Thomas (1996), *Meetings with Remarkable Trees*, Weidenfeld & Nicholson, London

Peattie, Donald Culross (1950), *The Natural History of Western Trees*, Houghton Mifflin Company, Boston

Pennant, Thomas (1771, edition 1998), *A Tour in Scotland in 1769*, Benjamin White, London

Perring, F.H. and Walters, S.M. (1976), *Atlas of the British Flora*, EP Publishing, Wakefield

Peterken, George F. (1996), *Natural Woodland*, Cambridge University Press, Cambridge

Quelch, Peter (2000), 'Expanding Native Woodland', *Reforesting Scotland* 23

Ramsay, P. (1997), *Revival of the Land: Creag Meagaidh National Nature Reserve*, Scottish Natural Heritage, Battleby, Perthshire

Ratcliffe, Derek (ed.) (1977), *A Nature Conservation Review*, Cambridge University Press, Cambridge

Read, Helen (1999), *Veteran Tree: A Guide to Good Management*, English Nature, Peterborough

Reid, John (1683), *The Scot's Gard'ner*, David Lindsay, Edinburgh

Richens, R.H. (1983), *Elm*, Cambridge University Press, Cambridge

Rodwell, J.S. and Patterson, G.S. (1994), 'Creating New Native Woodlands', *Forestry Commission Bulletin* 112, HMSO, London

Smout, Chris (1999), 'The History of Rothiemurchus Woodlands' in Smout, T. C. and Lambert, R. A. (eds.), *Rothiemurchus Nature and People on a Highland Estate 1500–2000*, Scottish Cultural Press, Edinburgh

Smout, T.C. (ed.) (1993), *Scotland since Prehistory*, Scottish Cultural Press, Aberdeen

Stell, Geoffrey and Baille, Michael (1993), 'The Great Hall and Roof of

Darnaway Castle', *Moray, Province and People,* The Scottish Society of Northern Studies, Edinburgh

Stewart, Katharine (2000), *Abriachan,* Abriachan Forest Trust, Abriachan

Stirling-Maxwell, J. (1929), *Loch Ossian Plantations,* privately printed

Strutt, Jacob George (1826), *Sylva Britannica or Portraits of Forest Trees Distinguished for their Antiquity, Magnitude or Beauty,* Henry G. Bohn, London

Taylor, Jenny (1995), *Orkney Native Tree Conservation Strategy,* privately printed

Walker, John (1808), 'A Catalogue of Some of the Most Considerable Trees in Scotland', in J. Walker (1812), *Essays on Natural History and Rural Economy,* University Press, Edinburgh

Walker, M.J.C., Merritt, J.W., et al (1992), 'Allt Odhar and Dalcharn: Two pre-Late Devensian/Weichselian sites in Northern Scotland', *Journal of Quarternary Science* 7

Wilson, E.H. (1913, edition of 1986), *A Naturalist in Western China,* Cadogan Books, London

Worrell, R., Gordon, A.G., Lee, R.S. and McInroy, A. (1999), 'Flowering and seed production of aspen in Scotland during a heavy seed year', *Forestry* 72

Zehetmayr, J.W.L. (1954), 'Experiments in Tree Planting on Peat', *Forestry Commission Bulletin* 22, HMSO, London

Zehetmayr, J.W.L. (1960), 'Afforestation of Upland Heaths', *Forestry Commission Bulletin* 32, HMSO, Edinburgh

USEFUL ADDRESSES

ORGANISATIONS EXCLUSIVELY CONCERNED WITH TREES:

Borders Forest Trust, Monteviot Nurseries, Ancrum, Jedburgh TD8 6TU

Central Scotland Countryside Trust, Hillhouseridge, Shottskirk Road, Shotts ML7 4JS

Forestry Commission, 231 Corstorphine Road, Edinburgh EH12 7AT

Highland Birchwoods, Littleburn, Munlochy, Ross-shire IV8 8NN

Institute of Chartered Foresters, 7a St Colme Street, Edinburgh EH3 6AA

Reforesting Scotland, 62–66 Newhaven Road, Edinburgh EH6 5QB

Royal Scottish Forestry Society, Hagg-on-Esk, Canonbie DG14 0XE

Scottish Forestry Trust, 5 Dublin Street Lane South, Edinburgh EH1 3PX

Scottish Native Woods, 3 Kenmore Street, Aberfeldy PH15 2BL

Timber Growers Association, 5 Dublin Street Lane South, Edinburgh EH1 3PX

The Woodland Trust, Glenruthven Mill, Abbey Road, Auchterarder PH3 1DP

ORGANISATIONS CONCERNED WITH TREES BUT NOT EXCLUSIVELY:

The Centre for Environmental History and Policy, University of St Andrews, St John's House, 65 South Street, St Andrews KY16 9QW

Deer Commission, 82 Fairfield Road, Inverness IV3 5LH

Historic Scotland, Longmore House, Salisbury Place, Edinburgh EH9 1SH

Institute of Terrestrial Ecology, Bush Estate, Penicuik, Midlothian EH26 0QB

National Farmers Union of Scotland, West Mains, Ingliston, Newbridge EH28 8LT

The National Trust for Scotland, 28 Charlotte Square, Edinburgh EH2 4ET

Royal Botanic Garden, Inverleith Row, Edinburgh EH3 5LR

Royal Society for the Protection of Birds, Dunedin House, 25 Ravelston Terrace, Edinburgh EH4 3TP

Scottish Environment Protection Agency, Erskine Court, The Castle Business Park, Stirling FK9 4TR

Scottish Executive, Rural Affairs Department, Pentland House, 47 Robb's Loan, Edinburgh EH14 1TY

Scottish Landowners Federation, Stuart House, Station Road, Musselburgh EH21 7PB

Scottish Natural Heritage, 12 Hope Terrace, Edinburgh EH12 9AS

Scottish Wildlife Trust, Cramond House, Cramond Glebe Road, Edinburgh EH4 6NS

World Wildlife Fund, 1 Crieff Road, Aberfeldy PH15 2BJ